**VOLUME TWENTY-ONE**


Book One
REGIME CHANGE AND THE
COHERENCE OF EUROPEAN GOVERNMENTS
Mark Irving Lichbach

Book Two
OUTCAST COUNTRIES
IN THE WORLD COMMUNITY
Efraim Inbar

# MONOGRAPH SERIES IN WORLD AFFAIRS

Graduate School of International Studies
University of Denver
Denver, Colorado 80208

Editor ........................................Karen A. Feste
Managing Editor..............................Millie Van Wyke

Send manuscripts in triplicate to Karen A. Feste, Editor, Monograph Series in World Affairs, Graduate School of International Studies, University of Denver, Denver, Colorado 80208. Manuscripts already published, scheduled for publication elsewhere, or simultaneously submitted to another journal are not acceptable.

# \ Outcast Countries
# in the World Community /
### Efraim Inbar

Volume 21
Book 2

Monograph Series in World Affairs
Graduate School of International Studies
University of Denver
Denver, Colorado 80208

**Library of Congress Cataloging in Publication Data**

Inbar, Efraim, 1947-
  Outcast countries in the world community.

  (Monograph series in world affairs ; v. 21, bk. 2)
  Bibliography: p.
  1. World politics—1965-1975. 2. World politics—1975-1985.
3. Israel—Foreign relations. 4. South Africa—Foreign
relations—1961-1978. 5. South Africa—Foreign relations—1978-
6. Taiwan—Foreign relations—1945-    . 7. Korea (South)—
Foreign relations. I. Title. II. Series.
D849.I493      1985          327'.09'04          84-28059
ISBN 0-87940-077-3

# ABOUT THE AUTHOR

Efraim Inbar is a Lecturer of Political Studies at Bar Ilan University. His research interests and previous publications concern Israeli national security and its foreign policy. Dr. Inbar holds a Ph.D. in Political Science from the University of Chicago.

To my Mother
Blessed be Her Memory

# ACKNOWLEDGMENTS

This work is a revised version of part of my Ph.D. dissertation. I would like to thank the members of my doctoral committee, Albert Wohlstetter, Leonard Binder and Lloyd I. Rudolph for their helpful comments. I benefited as well from the remarks of Saadia Touval, Yair Evron, Aaron Klieman, Shai Feldman and Shaul Stampfer. The criticisms of an anonymous reader of this Series and its editor were also well taken.

# TABLE OF CONTENTS

1. OUTCAST COUNTRIES .............................. 3
   Introduction ......................................... 3
2. THE EMERGENCE OF OUTCAST STATES
   IN WORLD POLITICS .............................. 11
   The Nature of Regional Conflict—Politicide .............. 11
   Marginality ........................................... 16
   Outcast States and the International System .............. 20
   Israel's Deteriorating International Position .............. 31
   Exit from Outcast Status ............................. 34
   Conclusion ........................................... 39
3. STRATEGIES ...................................... 41
   Strategy for Outcasts' Opponents ...................... 41
   Strategies for the Outcast State ....................... 54
4. CONCLUSION ...................................... 69
   REFERENCES ...................................... 81

# Outcast Countries
# in the World Community

# 1

## OUTCAST COUNTRIES

### Introduction

*Lo, it is a people that shall dwell alone, and shall not be reckoned among the nations.*
Balaam's Prophecy, Numbers 23:9

This work looks at an odd phenomenon in international politics of the post-World War II period—the outcast state. During this time, in different corners of the world, states emerged—Israel, South Africa, Taiwan and South Korea—that became increasingly isolated in the international system of the 1970s and 1980s. Apart from trying to understand the emergence of this phenomenon, this monograph attempts to clarify the security implications of isolation for these relatively small nations, the outcasts, which are usually not studied as a group.

Isolation is not a new phenomenon in international relations. Isolation in world politics, meaning that a state has little or no interaction with the rest of the actors in the international system, can originate in political processes within the lonely state or can result from other powers' actions. At times, Imperial China and Japan isolated themselves by deliberately minimizing their political and even cultural contacts with the outside world; the United States for years pursued an isolationist strategy. Temporary withdrawal from international affairs could also be the result of diverting national energy to internal affairs as happened, for example, in the People's Republic of China (PRC) during the Cultural Revolution. Civil wars or internal turmoil may paralyze the foreign policy of a country. Such consciously adopted or self-inflicted isolation is not dealt with here.

This research focuses on isolation imposed upon a state by other international actors. Many countries participated in the attempt to impose a *cordon sanitaire* upon the new Soviet regime after 1917, hoping the Communist government would collapse. Similarly, many democratic countries refrained from any interaction with Franco's Spain to express their resentment toward its Fascist regime.

3

This study limits the discussion to a distinct group of states that are isolated in the post-World War II international system and that share a particular type of regional conflict—politicide. "Politicide" is a campaign to destroy completely an existing political entity and can take the form of military and/or economic and/or political measures to eradicate the challenged state. The term was coined by Harkabi (1969) to describe the Palestinian goal of eliminating Israel. Outcast countries are isolated states that face a challenge to their mere existence, primarily at the regional level. Outcast status is characterized by two necessary conditions: (a) a state of international isolation; (b) a politicide campaign. The four countries studied together in this monograph belong to the outcast state category because they display both these characteristics.

Opponents of Israel, South Africa, Taiwan and South Korea try to eliminate the outcast state as an international actor by refusing to grant legitimacy to these states and by attempting to mobilize the international community to isolate them. This is different from trying to isolate a state in order to extract concessions in the form of territory, special rights or a change in policy. The outcasts' opponents have been somewhat successful in isolating their regional rivals.

Several ways to measure isolation are obvious. The first is the number of states that have diplomatic relations with the outcast country. Israel, South Africa, Taiwan and, to a lesser extent, South Korea, stand out in the international community with regard to their limited formal relations with other countries. South Africa has diplomatic relations with less than twenty states, while Taiwan maintains formal ties with less than thirty. Israel has a slightly broader network of diplomatic representation, while South Korea's formal ties with some sixty nations places it in the least isolated position of the four. Rather more significant than the number of embassies each outcast hosts in its country is the number of countries that have severed ties with the outcast or who refuse to have any formal contacts with them. Most countries in the world community consciously refrain from any dealings with the four outcasts. In terms of this criterion, there is no other country in a comparable position to the four outcasts.

A second criterion for measuring isolation is the membership of a state in International Governmental Organizations (IGOs). South Korea has never been accepted as a member of the United Nations (U.N.), Taiwan was expelled from this organization in 1971, and South Africa has been excluded from participating in the U.N. General Assembly and its organs since 1974. Israel's foes have attempted almost every year in the past decade to prevent its participation at the United Nations. Similarly, U.N.-affiliated agencies and regional IGOs are not hospitable to the four outcasts.

The third measure of isolation is the outcome of issues raised at the United Nations, its affiliated organizations and other international organizations, that relate to the outcasts. Each of the four outcasts has consistently fared very poorly in U.N. votes concerning issues of great consequence to its welfare. Taiwan has been expelled. South Africa is prevented from being an equal and active member and has been subjected to a continuous flow of anti-South African resolutions. Similarly, Israel is the subject of innumerable resolutions of condemnation; its national revival movement, Zionism, was condemned in 1975 as a form of racism, an act that undermined Israel's legitimacy. Here again, South Korea is in a better position, since it has been spared to a great extent the type of condemnations to which Israel and South Africa have been subject. This denotes a higher level of legitimacy. Nevertheless, primarily during its participation in the Vietnam War, South Korea has been subject to increasing international criticism, especially in communist and Third World forums.

Taking into consideration the three criteria suggested above, we can conclude quite clearly that the four countries, Israel, South Africa, South Korea and Taiwan, are isolated in the international community to a larger extent than any other international actor in the present system. Since the late 1960s, many countries have withdrawn diplomatic recognition from the outcast states. Others have severed their diplomatic relations. IGOs have increasingly passed resolutions against these international outcasts. Israel and South Africa in particular have become the subject of international moral condemnation. The outcast countries have been formally expelled from some international organizations and forums, or simply excluded from entry in others. Opponents of the outcast states have attempted to organize international sanctions or full-scale boycotts. In the case of South Africa, internationally organized military intervention has also been contemplated. These four states are treated similarly in the international system. This places them in a separate but not homogeneous category of international actors—the outcast states. [For a review of the magnitude of isolation as measured by the number of countries with which they maintain diplomatic relations and their identity, the outcomes of vital issues raised at the United Nations, and membership in international organizations, see Harkavy (1981:138-42). He was the first to treat these isolated states as a separate category of international actors (Harkavy, 1977:623-49). This section on isolation relies heavily on these two publications.]

To be classified as an outcast, it is clear that at least a majority of the international community must express displeasure with the outcast state by voting against its interests at IGOs and by refraining from formal ties with it. Furthermore, this pattern of conduct has to be maintained for some period of time. Some states experienced temporary status as an outcast: Uganda under Amin was not a very popular country and it was even occasionally condemned at international forums; Libya under Khadafy, or Khomeini's Iran have seemed to evoke some international criticism. Other examples of some degree of international isolation and/or international condemnation could be added, such as Kampuchea. In the present international constellation, however, no international actor has reached the extent of isolation experienced by the four outcasts. Furthermore, the peculiar regional conflict—politicide—which motivates the isolation drive, places these four countries in a separate category.

The desire to destroy a political entity for political, economic or normative reasons is not new. History has witnessed the rise and the destruction of many states. The tribes of Israel tried to eradicate the people of Amalek. The Romans ploughed Carthage and Corinth under to obliterate traditional centers of anti-Roman leadership. Poland was dismantled several times. Various religious wars against "infidels" are historic precedents of the normative aspect of politicide.

Yet in the twentieth century, particularly in the post-World War II period, the drive for politicide is a unique political behavior. It has been argued that the evolution of liberalism, democracy, national self-determination and international law has partially or directly enhanced the chances of small powers to maintain their precarious independence in the face of threats from the great powers (Wright, 1957, 1964). The threat to the existence of isolated small states is particularly intriguing since it comes not so much from the superpowers as from less powerful regional adversaries.

For some time after World War II, several states in addition to the four above-mentioned outcasts faced a similar liquidation campaign. The most notable example was Communist China; Taiwan claimed to represent all China and hoped to overthrow the "illegitimate" Communist regime. Taiwan's campaign was successful for some time primarily because the United States supported its claim and lent its political weight to prevent the recognition and establishment of diplomatic relations with Peking. It is remarkable that the PRC gained entrance to the United Nations only in 1971. East Germany was similarly ostracized as a result of the efforts on the part of West Germany. The "Hallstein Doctrine" adopted officially on 9 December 1955 announced that the German Federal Republic would break relations with all countries that recognized the East German regime. In this instance the Soviet Union was made the exception.

Not only communist countries faced attempts to prevent their acceptance into the international community. For a shorter period, Mauritania and Kuwait suffered from the outcast condition. Their neighbors, Morocco and to a lesser extent Mali in the first case, and Iraq in the second case, refused to accept the existence of the newly established state and wanted to annex it. For several years both Mauritania and Kuwait were refused membership in the United Nations primarily because the Soviet Union supported the irredentist claims of Morocco and Iraq (Touval, 1972; Shimoni and Levine, 1974). These four countries, however, succeeded in overcoming the politicide drive. Another difference is that the present outcasts were accepted members of the international community that underwent a process of isolation, while the PRC, East Germany, Mauritania and Kuwait faced international isolation at their establishment. Although these countries do not presently qualify as outcast states, they serve as points of reference to elucidate some of the issues concerning outcast status.

Among the outcasts in this study, Israel draws the most attention; yet the discussion relates also to the situation and experience of the three other outcasts. The methodology is a "comparative case study" approach. Obviously there are limitations to such an approach since the differences among the four outcasts are not minimal. Nevertheless, the basic situation of outcast status is similar. This work claims that this situation stems from systemic factors; therefore, a systemic analysis allows us to arrive at generalizations concerning the outcast state phenomenon. Furthermore, in the absence of controlled comparisons, there is no other alternative to the comparative case study approach if we want to deal at the general level with the reasons for acquiring an outcast status and with the influence this shared specific situation has on the national security of the outcasts.

Investigation into the outcast state clarifies some of the issues regarding this type of state in a particular set of systemic conditions. In discussing the success of the outcasts' foes in mobilizing international support for their isolating efforts, this study elaborates on related phenomena such as coalition dynamics and global interdependence in a loosened bipolar system. It enhances our understanding of the present international system.

7

This study analyzes the reasons why South Africa, South Korea, Taiwan and Israel became outcast states more or less simultaneously. The emergence of several outcast states within a short time, between the late 1960s and early 1970s, suggests that their new status stems not only from common regional politicide campaigns and some national characteristics, but also from global developments. It is argued that the outcasts' rivals emerged from upheavals in the international system during this period with greater political leverage than before, which enabled them to mobilize international support to increase the isolation of the outcast states. The loosening of bipolarity, the emergence of a better-coordinated Third World and the decline of the United States as a global power weakened the status of the outcast states. The outcasts were allied with an America in retreat, while their opponents were communists or belonged to the Third World coalition. This work claims, therefore, that the systemic circumstances are the most relevant in explaining the reasons for acquiring outcast status, and also for escaping this condition.

A second issue to be clarified in this study is the effect of the outcasts' new international status on their national security, and on the strategies available to change this condition or to alleviate the difficulties arising from the newly acquired status. The diplomatic, economic and military consequences of the outcast condition are assessed. The intensity of the regional conflict and its global linkages are the parameters defining the limits within which a viable strategy can be formulated and executed. Relations with its reluctant ally and major weapons supplier, the United States, are shown to be a critical element in the outcast's national security. The implications of the increasing uncertainty as to U.S. political and material support are a primary consideration in devising national strategies.

Since the outcast states are small, this study contributes to the inquiry into small state behavior. The capacity of a small state to withstand a long-range regional conflict accompanied by international isolation is assessed. In addition, the small state alliance with a major power is an important issue dealt with in this essay. This work relies on the small state studies and hopefully will become a valued addition to the burgeoning body of the small state literature.

This study also draws conceptually from the strategic studies literature. The outcast states face military threats of various kinds. Furthermore, they face a powerful campaign to isolate them and to weaken their ties with their major ally—the United States. Several alternative strategies are suggested to cope with the outcast state predicament. In a similar vein to many strategic studies, this work is also prescriptive in that it points to a preferred strategy for the outcast state.

In general terms, the purpose of this monograph is to probe into an interesting phenomenon in the contemporary international system—the outcast state. In the treatment of this subject, several aspects of inter-state relations beyond the outcast state issue are also illuminated.

# 2

## THE EMERGENCE OF OUTCAST STATES
## IN WORLD POLITICS

This chapter addresses three questions: Why did Israel, like South Africa, Taiwan and South Korea, and unlike other states, acquire outcast status? Why did these states become isolated at a particular time? Under what circumstances can the isolation process be reversed? The answers to these questions are not unrelated. All outcasts fell into their positions as a result of changes in the international system and could do little to prevent it. The simultaneous emergence of several outcast states at the end of the 1960s and beginning of the 1970s, in different regions, suggests that their new status does stem from global developments in addition to the common characteristic of the regional conflict (politicide) and the similarities in their national strategic and ethno-cultural qualities. This chapter focuses, however, on the process by which Israel has become an outcast and discusses the possibilities of exiting from the situation.

### THE NATURE OF REGIONAL CONFLICT—POLITICIDE

The most striking common characteristic of an outcast state is the nature of its regional conflicts. It is not the usual inter-state conflict over limited goals (which still can be fought as a total war), but over the mere existence of the outcast state. This is a "right to life" issue. In spite of the fact that the present international system displays heterogeneity with regard to the principle of legitimacy, the form of state and social structure (Aron, 1966), the most visible mutual characteristic of the outcast state in the international political community is the challenge to its legitimacy.

In international relations, the term "legitimacy" is ambiguous. It has a descriptive as well as a normative meaning. In the descriptive sense, a state meets the criterion of legitimacy if its government has a monopoly of power in its territory. In a normative sense, the criterion for recognizing a state's legitimacy is the nature of the regime and/or the way in which it came to power. The recognition of a state's legitimacy, i.e., the monopoly of power over a certain territory, does not necessarily imply normative approval as well. On the other hand, governments sometimes refuse to acknowledge the legitimacy of a state, in spite of the fact that it is legitimate in the descriptive sense, for bargaining purposes, or in order to challenge its existence. The acknowledgment of legitimacy is therefore also an instrument of policy. Similarly, establishing or severing diplomatic relations with a country are policy acts. The motivation for such steps may or may not be normative. Today states express disapproval by mixing nonrecognition with different combinations of limits to contact. The greater the level of ideological conflict, the more political use is made of recognitions of legitimacy (Peterson, 1982:324-52). Yet because of the ambiguity of the term "legitimacy," the meaning of such actions is determined primarily by situational factors.

The Arab refusal to recognize Israel is primarily motivated by the widespread belief in the Arab world that the existence of the Jewish state is illegitimate. It is argued that Israel is an artificial state, since the Jews are not a nation but a religious sect with no collective political rights. Furthermore, the establishment of Israel was the result of a Western imperialistic scheme. Arab hostility toward the Jewish state is also rooted in Islamic culture. Although classic Muslim writings contain many anti-Jewish expressions, the traditional Muslim attitude to Jews has been ambivalent: cultural affinity exists along with a belief in Arab religious and political superiority. As the Arab-Israeli conflict evolved, the anti-Jewish motifs of this tradition have been emphasized. Furthermore, elements of Christian European anti-Semitism and even anti-Zionist ideals of the radical left were absorbed into an anti-Jewish ideology. The image of the Jew as evil and as a danger to the Arab world as well as to human civilization has been propagated by official Arab organs. According to this ideology, the only rational and moral alternative has been the liquidation of the Jewish state. (For the most comprehensive exposition of this view, see Harkabi, 1972, 1977; see also Maoz, 1976.)

The Arab countries have conducted a diplomatic campaign against Israel, primarily in order to challenge its existence, even though bargaining elements versus Israel or extra-regional powers have not been absent. The diplomatic drive has complemented, and for periods of time substituted for, military activity in an effort to achieve the goal of eliminating the Jewish state through politicide. The intensity of pursuing this objective has oscillated over time. The ruling elites in Arab countries also have other goals. In spite of their great commitment to the destruction of Israel, they are sensitive to the price involved in such an endeavor.

Politicide as the final Arab objective has been obscured in recent years. Following the Arabs' defeat in the 1967 war, new modes of thinking about the Arab-Israeli conflict have emerged. Many Arabs have adopted an incremental approach, emphasizing concrete demands on Israel, such as withdrawal to the 1967 territorial lines and the establishment of a Palestinian state in the West Bank, rather than focusing attention on politicide. As a general objective, politicide has not helped in marshalling international support for the Arab cause, although it remains the preferred goal of most Arab countries. One school of thought, which seems to be held by "moderate" Arab statesmen, calls for "reducing Israel to its natural dimensions" (the phrase is Harkabi's), but it is ambiguous as to what may happen after the Arab demands are met. Its open-endedness may be viewed as an effort to allay suspicions of Arab extremists, or as a plot to weaken Israel, rather than as coexistence. (For a schematic presentation of the three main trends of post-1967 Arab thought, see Harkabi, 1977.)

In any case, the Arab countries, with the possible exception of Egypt, have not yet accepted the *right* of the Jews to self-determination in any part of the land called Palestine. President Sadat during his trip to Jerusalem (November 1977) explicitly accepted the legitimacy of the Israeli government only in the descriptive sense. He said, "Israel has become a fait accompli recognized by the world" (Sadat, 1978). In the March 1979 peace treaty, Egypt and Israel declared, however, that they recognized and will respect each other's right to live in peace within secure and recognized borders (Article III:ib). This paragraph does not fully indicate a normative inclination to accept Israel. There is widespread opposition to the reconciliation with Israel. Indeed, many of the Egyptian political and intellectual elite still view the Jews as a religious sect, rather than as a national entity. (For a report of such views, see "Egyptian-Israeli Dialogue," *Maariv,* 23 January 1981.) In fact, an increasing discontent with Egyptian-Israeli relations is discernible in Egypt today (Monen Al Mashet, 1983). The intensity of opposition to the 1978 Camp David accords and the 1979 Egyptian-Israeli treaty varies in the Arab world. Yet the reluctance to accept peace with Israel unites all Arab countries, moderate and radical, Oman being the notable exception (Meddy-Weitzman, 1980). What some consider signs of moderation in several Arab countries do not exist at the normative level.

Nevertheless, temporary accommodations are not precluded, as the periods of nonviolence or low intensity of violence indicate. Nor is it ruled out that a temporary agreement may acquire permanency over time. (Permanence, in political discourse, is a relative term.) Meanwhile, however, the existence of Israel, like the existence of the other outcast states in their present character, is incompatible with the vision of the future held by its neighbors. On paper, the sub-Sahara African nations seem to want only the abolition of the racist policies of the South African government and implementation of majority rule democracy, which would mean black rule. Such a desire probably stems from sincere compassion for oppressed blacks. Yet there is also an underlying refusal to accept the separate existence of a white nation in South Africa, now tragically mixed with nonwhite natives and immigrants. The refusal to accept the South African whites' claim that they are a separate nation with collective political rights (as distinct from individual rights) is the main argument for politicide. The claim to be a separate tribe is what distinguished the whites in Rhodesia from the whites in South Africa. Those in Rhodesia did not claim to be a distinct national entity with legitimate collective political rights. They were primarily concerned with their individual rights within the boundaries of post-British-ruled Rhodesia. The emergence of Zimbabwe was never portrayed as the destruction of the white nation in Rhodesia. In South Africa, however, there is a much larger white community than in Rhodesia. Moreover, the South African white community considers itself a "white tribe" with legitimate collective political rights. Like the Jews of Israel, they are ethnically and culturally different from their neighbors; neither group is accepted as a separate national entity.

Taiwan and South Korea are in a somewhat different position. South Korea, explicitly, and Taiwan, implicitly, are willing to forego the goal of national unification and to accept a "German formula" of partition. South Korea has accepted a two-Koreas representation arrangement at the United Nations, but North Korea's friends have blocked it. [For a de facto willingness for a "German formula" in the Republic of China (ROC), see Li and Lewis, 1977.] This is not satisfactory to Peking or Pyongyang. Taiwan and South Korea are anathema to China and North Korea, respectively, which pursue a more militant policy for national unification. The fact that part of their own people have succeeded in maintaining a noncommunist alternative is seen as a challenge to the legitimacy of the communist states. Indeed, both countries have consistently argued that should a peaceful unification no longer appear feasible, the use of force would then be undertaken. The Taiwanese and the South Koreans, in contrast to the Jews in Israel and the whites in

South Africa, are identified culturally and ethnically with the population of their opponents. The peoples of Taiwan and South Korea are not threatened with national extinction. Their states, not their people, have outcast status.

Table 1 illustrates the difference in the normative character of the politicide campaigns against the four outcasts. The Arab opponents, notably Syria, Libya and the Palestine Liberation Organization (PLO) —the rejectionist front—deny the Jews' right to self-determination. The Jewish state is viewed as a historic aberration and its regime is labeled as racist. As a result, expulsion of its Jewish residents is also considered among Arab aims, as article 6 of the Palestinian National Covenant suggests (Harkabi, 1974:53-55). In the case of South Africa, the political framework as a state is not challenged, only its regime—apartheid. Yet at the same time the whites are required to disappear as a separate "tribe." The Taiwanese and South Koreans are required, however, only to relinquish their separate state and their non-communist regime. Table 1 indicates that the normative aspect of politicide is more far-reaching in the case of Israel than in the case of the other outcasts.

**Table 1**
**Normative Dimensions of Outcast Status**

| Country | Lack of Legitimacy to | Regime | State | People |
|---------|----------------------|--------|-------|--------|
| Israel | | + | + | + |
| South Africa | | + | | + |
| Taiwan | | + | + | |
| South Korea | | + | + | |

It should be pointed out that the struggle against the outcast states is not limited to the diplomatic level. Each state also faces a military threat whose effectiveness is subject to changes in intranational, regional and global circumstances. Israel has fought six wars since 1948 and the Arabs have not given up the military option "to liberate the Arab territories and to restore the legitimate rights of the Palestinian people" (a vague formula which is sometimes used as a euphemism for the destruction of Israel) (Harkavy, 1977:627-39). The independence of

Mozambique and Angola following the 1974 Portuguese revolution left South Africa psychologically and physically more exposed when these buffers against the threat of black nationalism disappeared (Barrat, 1976b). A similar effect was produced by the fall of the white regime in Rhodesia. The support of guerrilla warfare in South Africa, carried out by the Liberation Committee of the Organization of African Unity (OAU), has therefore become easier. The PRC is not willing to relinquish the option of annexing Taiwan by force, if necessary. North Korea similarly reserves the right to invade the southern part of the Korean peninsula.

The actual level of violence against the outcast varies according to its opponents' military and political capabilities. Yet all campaigns take the character of what Speier (1952) calls an "absolute war," as distinguished from instrumental, agonistic war (for the sake of the game or glory). In an absolute war, the enemy, be it the regime, the state or the people, must be totally destroyed.

## MARGINALITY

Apart from being subject to a campaign of politicide, Israel and the other outcast states share some forms of marginality that affect their fortunes in the international arena. First, those states seem to have in common a strategic marginality, i.e., no consensus exists as to their strategic importance to their Western allies. The evaluation of their strategic contribution fluctuates according to changing international circumstances. A second form of marginality is their ethno-cultural features, not entirely Western, which reinforce their strategic marginality.

### Strategic Marginality

Israel, because of its location at the crossroads of three continents, is situated geographically in a place of strategic importance. But so is Egypt. Moreover, a comparison between small Israel and the many Arab countries with their potential illuminates the problematic nature of siding with Israel. Indeed, the United States' diplomatic history in the Middle East does not show consistent support for Israel (Bryson, 1977; Quandt, 1977). Israel is definitely a strategic asset to the United States, but after 1973 a costly one. The anti-Western turn of Iran in 1979 seemed to enhance Israel's strategic importance for the West, but the rising Islamic wave again pointed out the difficulties involved in being allied with the Jewish state. The growing Western interest in and dependence upon Middle Eastern oil accentuated Israel's strategic marginality.

In contrast, the strategic marginality of the other outcast states became clearer when the United States' scope of interest narrowed. Immediately after World War II, neither the retreating nationalist Chinese regime nor South Korea was clearly within the "perimeter" of American national interest. They have gained importance only as a result of the cold war. The American-Chinese detente seems to have reduced the importance of Taiwan and South Korea as outposts for containing Chinese Communism. Taiwan, which had a formal defense treaty with the United States, had to rely on an increasingly reluctant ally. The South Vietnamese pullout in 1975 underscored American weakness and increased Taiwanese apprehension about the trustworthiness of the United States as an ally. The withdrawal of recognition of Taiwan by the United States in December 1978 finally shattered any illusions left about the course of American foreign policy in the area.

Developments in East Asia and South Asia similarly affected South Korea. American plans for withdrawal from the Korean peninsula, which were later changed, indicated the questionable strategic importance attached to the area. Japan shares the South Korean apprehensions, and favors continued American presence. Interestingly, neither the Chinese nor the Russians are eager to see the Americans out of South Korea, since such an American move could change the balance of power in the region (Bedeski, 1983:6-7; McLane, 1973:10-14). Nonetheless, the American presence in South Korea, attacked often in international forums, is becoming less palatable in the United States. Some Americans even claim that North Korea is the one displaying flexibility and that the U.S. contingent in South Korea constitutes the obstacle to peace (Porter, 1979; Reischauer, 1974).

South Africans view their country as an indispensable bulwark for Western civilization against the threat of communism. Yet the South African claim for incorporation into the structure of the Western alliance has appeared to be low on the Western list of strategic priorities. The Angolan civil war demonstrated to South Africa what Vietnam indicated to Taiwan and South Korea—American hesitation to intervene in areas redefined as being of little importance. The South African foreign minister, in a speech to parliament on 26 April 1976, said: "Angola has demonstrated that in times of crisis we cannot rely on the West in general and on the United States in particular, and that at least we know where we stand now" (Barrat, 1976:153).

The strategic importance attributed by the United States to non-European regions fluctuates according to international circumstances. Changes in the international system that are unfavorable, from the outcasts' point of view, are discussed later; at this time, the discussion turns to internal characteristics that contribute to outcast states' strategic marginality.

**Ethno-Cultural Marginality**

The concept of the "marginal man" as someone living and sharing intimately in the cultural life and traditions of two distinct peoples, never quite willing to break with his past and his traditions but not quite accepted, because of racial prejudices, in the new society (Park, 1928:881-93), was later applied to groups of people sharing the same cultural marginality (Goldberg, 1940:52-58; Antonovsky, 1956:57-62). In this study, the notion of marginality is used in a looser sense; it notes that ethno-cultural integration of the outcast state with its political allies, as well as with its geographic environment, is only a partial integration.

Outcast states are formal or informal allies of the United States, but because they are not fully Western, it is easier for the West to detach itself from their destinies. The new American isolationists, in contrast to the old, want to disengage only from Asia. The commitment to Europe is not like that to other parts of the world; it is based upon racial and cultural affinity (Tucker, 1972; Schurman, 1977).

Israel, although it emerged as a Western society, is a Middle Eastern (Asian) nation in terms of geographic location, language and, to a large extent, ethnic origin. In addition, Israel is Jewish. In many instances, traditional anti-Semitism takes the form of anti-Zionist or anti-Israeli attitudes.

Similarly, it is easier to desert South Africa than Europe. True, South Africa is ruled by whites, but it is not in Europe. Moreover, the relation between the metropolis and the white colonists is charged with ambivalence (Mannoni, 1964). Taiwan and South Korea are Asian allies, in spite of their more successful adaptation to Western culture and its modes of production.

Interestingly, the Western democracies seem to have developed a lower tolerance for abuses of human rights in the outcast states than elsewhere. The West seems unable to sort out facts in its adversaries' propaganda (Moynihan, 1979:1-10). For example, Israel, one of few democracies outside the Atlantic alliance, is criticized for holding territories occupied in 1967 (which include nearly one million Arabs). No democracy is to be found in the Arab world surrounding Israel, nor is great respect for human rights. Objections are raised against Taiwan for not being a democracy, and aid for the authoritarian regime in Seoul has become increasingly controversial in the United States. Yet both Taiwan and South Korea grant their citizens greater freedom than do their totalitarian enemies. South Africa's racial policies are indeed repugnant. Yet this form of oppression seems to be singled out as intolerable, rather than grouped with other types of tyranny in sub-Sahara Africa or in other parts of the world.

Israel and South Africa are similarly rejected by their regional enemies on ethno-cultural grounds. The Middle East is predominantly Arab and Muslim. In contrast, Israel is Jewish and, culturally, the governing elite is Western-oriented. [Although there are many Oriental-Sephardic Jews in Israel, economic and political control is in the hands of Ashkenazi (European) Jews.] South Africa similarly stands out in terms of race and culture in sub-Sahara Africa.

Taiwan and South Korea are ethnically and culturally not very different from their opponents. Yet they are more Westernized in terms of economic and cultural style. Interestingly, Korea and Taiwan display some marginality even in terms of Asian culture. They have been in between the Chinese and the Japanese spheres of influence; both have experienced an anticolonialist struggle against the Japanese. This anticolonialist experience is also shared by Israel and South Africa, both of whom were against the British.

The outcast states are also rejected by most Third World countries. A Third World perspective divides the universe according to selected characteristics into two groups—members of the Third World, and all others. Among the criteria for defining membership are national wealth, degree of economic development, race and culture, ideology and rhetoric. While Israel, South Korea and Taiwan actually qualify on some scales of measurement as developing nations, they are not viewed as members of the club because they are seen by the Third World as too Western. The Third World identifies Israel and South Africa as Western countries in terms of race and culture. South Korea and Taiwan are politically identified as belonging to the Western camp.

Israel, South Korea and Taiwan are not rich countries, but they are not seen as belonging to the "have-nots." All are expanding industrial nations with a rather high standard of living. Ideologically and in terms of the rhetoric used, these four countries do not fall into the Third World preference. Israel's socialist orientation has been eclipsed by its being a Western liberal democracy. South Korea, Taiwan and South Africa are vehemently anticommunist. South Africa is, in addition, a white supremacy regime. Such crude images have always served as salient points for political activity (Rosenau, 1971:382).

The ethno-cultural marginality of the outcast is, under the international circumstances of the 1960s and 1970s, detrimental to its status in the West, as well as in the non-Western parts of the world. But marginality is not always detrimental; under certain political circumstances it may be beneficial. Yugoslavia's marginality, for example, continues to be an asset for its independence. It lies at the margins of the Slav, now Communist, empire, as well as at the fringes of Western Europe. Marginal groups are, however, more susceptible to changing political fortunes.

## OUTCAST STATES AND THE INTERNATIONAL SYSTEM

The outcast's marginality and the uncompromising regional hostility toward it have been constant factors in molding its position in the international system. An ongoing politicide campaign is a necessary condition for ostracizing a state. Yet it is not sufficient to "endow" a state with outcast status. Minimum international cooperation is needed for such a task. The timing of the international campaign to ostracize certain states is therefore intriguing; Israel, Taiwan and South Korea have been in continuous conflict with their neighbors since the late 1940s. Why were they to emerge, together with South Africa, as international outcasts only at the end of the 1960s and the early 1970s? Most Communist countries severed relations with Israel after the June 1967 war. Most of the African countries broke relations with Israel in the early 1970s (especially after the October 1973 war) and were joined in this by several Asian and Latin American countries. One obvious answer to the timing of this isolation process is the increased power of some Arab countries in world politics: (1) Egypt under Nasser emerged as one of the Third World leaders in the 1960s, (2) Saudi Arabia, owing to its huge oil reserves and formidable wealth, became an important international actor in the 1970s, and (3) in the energy-thirsty world, Arab oil-producing nations carried greater weight than before. Iraq and Libya, oil exporters and among the most uncompromising enemies of the "Zionist entity," also gained international prominence.

Similarly, the ostracizing of Taiwan is connected with the ascendancy of the PRC in international affairs. The reactivation of China's foreign policy after the end of the Cultural Revolution in 1968 made Taiwan's position less tenable. The years between 1970 and 1973 were particularly traumatic for Taiwan. The American-Chinese detente started and Taiwan was ousted from the United Nations (1971). In those years, twenty-eight countries severed diplomatic relations with Taiwan (Selya, 1975:441). In 1977, of the 155 countries in the world, only twenty-five maintained diplomatic relations with Taipei. In 1978, the United States also withdrew its recognition, constituting the most dramatic diplomatic setback of all.

Growing Chinese activity, particularly in Third World countries, also helped her neighbor, North Korea, in the drive for international recognition, as well as in her efforts to undermine South Korea's international position. South Korea is, however, least isolated among the outcasts. It has relations with over sixty nations, due in part to the relatively unimportant role of the North Koreans in world politics. Nevertheless, the North Korean diplomatic offensive has scored several successes in the last two decades: several countries have severed diplomatic relations with South Korea, and both Third World forums and some U.N. bodies have excluded it from membership. South Korea's participation in the Vietnam War and expanding United States military aid to Seoul (the American quid pro quo) triggered a great propaganda and diplomatic effort on the part of North Korea aimed at isolating and condemning South Korea as a "lackey of American imperialism" and arousing international opinion, particularly in the Third World, against the United States' continued military presence there. North Korea sought to position itself as the most reliable anti-colonial, anti-imperialist friend of the small developing nations. Since 1969, North Korean foreign policy has stressed Korean unification more than before and its bellicosity toward South Korea has not been as constant as before (Shinn, 1973:55-71; Roger, 1975:116-17). This ambivalence in North Korean foreign policy, unification via bilateral negotiations versus delegitimization of the South Korean regime, also eased the South Korean international position. The need not to estrange South Korea in its bilateral negotiations made the North Korean anti-South Korea campaign less extreme and less effective. In contrast to North Korea's policies, the PRC offered unification negotiations to Taiwan only after the latter lost American diplomatic support.

Likewise, South Africa's isolation is related to the emergence and the growing power of regional opponents to its apartheid. In the 1960s, numerous African colonies received independence and the new black nations became the largest voting block in most IGOs. Moreover, some of these countries have gained greater influence in international affairs as a result of their minerals or oil resources, Nigeria being the most notable example. Furthermore, the Republic of South Africa has traditionally favored an isolationist posture in foreign affairs and it has never developed a worldwide diplomatic network as did Israel and Taiwan. In 1965, South Africa had only two diplomatic missions in Asia (Japan and Lebanon) and only two in South America (Argentina and Brazil) in addition to representatives in the United States and Western Europe. It could not, therefore, be subject to dramatic severance of diplomatic relations. Yet, at that time, South Africa did participate in many international organizations; since the 1960s, however, it has been expelled, suspended, or has withdrawn from them under pressure from its African rivals.

The timing of the isolation of Israel and the other outcasts also entails a global perspective since the outcast status emerged as a result of actions at the interregional and global level. It is argued that in addition to the growing power of the outcast's rivals, the main reasons for the emergence of Israel and the other three countries as outcasts are (1) the loosening of bipolarity, (2) the retreat of American power, and (3) the increased cooperation and influence of Third World states.

**Loosening Bipolarity**
The major characteristic of international politics in the post-World War II period has been bipolarity, which denotes the dominance of the United States-Soviet Union relationship. The superpowers, as they were soon called (primarily because of their unsurpassable potential to destroy any enemy with their nuclear arsenals, and also because of their global military and economic reach) each led a bloc of aligned countries. The international system has, however, never been "tight bipolar" (Kaplan, 1957:43). First, there exist many nonaligned nations, whose numbers have increased mainly because of decolonization. Second, there are several dimensions to international politics—strategic, ideological, economic, diplomatic. Competition between states takes place, therefore, on several levels—chessboards, in Hoffman's (1970:401) language, where each chessboard has rules of its own, but is linked to the others. With the exception of the strategic level, referring to primarily effective nuclear capability, the other levels of international action display increasing multipolarity. The amount of leverage a country has over the outcome of international contingencies increasingly depends on the specific international problem, rather than on its status in the bipolar system.

At these levels, the challenges to which a superpower like the United States can adequately respond, by what Morgenthau (1960:130) called "unequivocal acts," have clearly diminished. The limits on the superpowers are due in the first place to the difficulty in using nuclear weapons, which results in a certain freedom for the middle and small powers. Moreover, there are inherent limits to the politico-military might of any power to control unstable societies and to effectively oppose revolutionary warfare (Knorr, 1966; Hoffman, 1968:52-83).

Therefore, the alliance of an outcast nation with the United States, one of the superpowers, has become a weak shield against hostile actions taken by the outcast's opponents, if those actions do not directly affect the United States-Soviet balance of power.

## The Retreat of American Power

In addition, there is a decline in the global power of the United States, not to be confused with the loosening of the international system (Waltz, 1967:215-31; Laqueur, 1975:44-52). The Nixon Doctrine, officially enunciated in July 1969, can be viewed as the United States' recognition of the new international circumstances and as heralding the retreat of American power. The United States redefined its global interests more narrowly as its isolationist predisposition became stronger. It has been suggested that a curious symbiosis of perceptions for a reduced American role emerged as the intellectual and business elites converged in their desire for less American involvement (Berger, 1976:23-27). Concomitantly, the Western alliance "loosened," underscoring the divergence of interests among its members. The United States faced greater difficulties in attempting to rally Western Europe behind its policies (Laqueur, 1980:21-27; Draper, 1981:13-69; Serfaty, 1981:70-86).

The lessening of bipolarity, reduced American involvement and international changes in various regions increased the autonomy of many national actors in regional systems such as Europe, South Asia and East Asia. Yet the outcast states seem less able to increase their freedom of action under these circumstances. Their marginality and their regional conflict against numerous countries (in the cases of Israel and South Africa) or against communist countries (in the cases of Taiwan and South Korea) who enjoy broad support, deny them political maneuverability and make them actually more dependent upon a weakened United States.

The loosening of the East Asian subsystem and the growing ambiguity surrounding the American commitment to its allies in that area explain the exposed position of Taiwan and South Korea and the improved leverage of the PRC and even North Korea. Similarly, the emergence of numerous black states in the African continent and the deterioration of the previously unchallenged Western position in Africa made the South African Republic more vulnerable.

Yet it is not clear that such evolution of outcast status took place with regard to Israel. The Middle East has never been a "tight bipolar" region. It has never been neatly divided into American and Soviet spheres of influence. Local American allies, as well as Soviet allies, have displayed independent courses of action. Moreover, Israel became more isolated when the influence of the United States in the area seemed to increase following the 1973 war. U.S.-USSR competition has not been the dominant factor in the relations of conflict and cooperation among the Middle Eastern states. The most important dimensions of the regional politics here are the inter-Arab rivalry and the Arab-Israeli conflict. The limited bipolar dimension enhanced the autonomy of regional actors and also eased superpowers' intervention (Binder, 1958:408-29).

In 1947 the United States and the Soviet Union voted in favor of establishing a Jewish state. The Soviet Union probably helped the new state in order to weaken the British Empire (Dagan, 1970:19-27). Until mid-1955, the Soviet Union was relatively inactive in the Middle East. Egyptian and Syrian leaders then invited the Soviet Union to their countries to counter American presence in rival Arab countries that the United States had organized into an anti-Soviet defense pact (the Baghdad Pact had concluded in February 1955). The desire to gain a source of modern military equipment to satisfy the military and to fight Israel was also a factor in the new Arab-Soviet relationship. Since 1955, partly because of the radicalization of several Arab countries, the United States' influence in the region has been reduced, which benefited the Soviet Union. The Soviet Union was interested in denying the strategically located and oil-rich Middle East to the West and in securing access to the Mediterranean and the Indian Ocean. The inter-Arab disputes facilitated Soviet penetration. The Soviet Union, however, preferred to be less vulnerable to fluctuations in Arab enmities and added a more permanent dimension to its presence in the Middle East by championing the Arab cause against Israel, the one issue that unifies all Arabs (Klieman, 1970; Freedman, 1975).

After the 1967 war, the Soviet commitment to Syria and especially to Egypt increased considerably. Following the war, Soviet propaganda also greatly intensified (Hazan, 1976). Israel was, of course, linked to United States' interests, and the nature of the "anti-imperialist struggle" was emphasized. This suited the Arab images of the conflict well. It seems that "seldom has the Soviet propaganda conducted an international campaign so zealously and intensively. Virtually all instruments of international propaganda have been mobilized to battle Zionism" (Hazan, 1976:154).

In 1970, the Soviets had 20,000 military personnel stationed in Egypt. Some of them even took an active part in the defense of Egypt against the Israelis, as combatants flying interceptors and manning surface-to-air missiles. Furthermore, in October 1973, the Soviet Union did not hesitate to replenish Egyptian and Syrian military stocks via an airlift, despite the possibility of deterioration of detente with the United States.

Early Soviet successes in the Arab world did not influence the United States to take a more pro-Israeli direction in its Middle East policy. The United States initially preferred not to be viewed as Israel's ally or protector; it even imposed an arms embargo on Israel until 1962. In the 1950s, Israel was also left out of the American-sponsored regional alliance. The Egyptian-Soviet friendship did not prevent the United States from pressuring Israel to withdraw from the Sinai following the 1956 Anglo-French-Israeli attack on Egypt.

Gradually, however, the United States became the major supplier of military hardware to Israel. After the successful war in 1967, Israel became viewed in the United States, though not unanimously, as having a balancing role in the Middle East. Already in 1957-1958, the United States observed that Israel's presence restricted Nasser's freedom of action by tying down the bulk of Egyptian forces, and prevented the regional struggles from assuming the character of military conflicts that would entangle the big powers (Safran, 1978:360).

Since 1967, the United States has perceived Israel as an effective barrier to the Soviet threat in the core area of the Middle East. The 1970 Jordanian crisis, in which Israeli forces deterred a greater Syrian effort to undermine the pro-Western Hashemite regime, further strengthened this perception. The issues of dispute between Israel and the United States—the character of a Middle East settlement, the American role in it and the scope of United States aid to Middle Eastern countries—were temporarily set aside. Moreover, the growing Soviet commitment to Egypt and Syria triggered a similar commitment on the part of the United States to Israel, in spite of their differences (Slonim, 1974).

In this sense, in the 1967-1973 period, the Arab-Israeli region was more bipolar than ever before. The United States' airlift of military aid to Israel in the October 1973 war was probably a response to a perceived lack of moderation on the part of the Soviet Union rather than to developments on the battlefield (Sheehan, 1976:13). The bipolar dimension was dramatically stressed when the United States placed its forces on alert on 25 October 1973, in reaction to Soviet military moves.

Yet the post-1973 period has been characterized, primarily because of Egypt's efforts, by a loosening of the bipolar dimension. Egypt's President Sadat adopted a notably less radical stance than his predecessor, Nasser. Internally, Sadat tried to liberalize the economy and to some extent the political structure. In foreign affairs, Egypt tried to court the

Americans. In 1972, Sadat even expelled the Soviet contingent (not only for this reason), but the United States did not respond since it was busy with its presidential election and subsequently with the Israeli elections (Quandt, 1977). After the October 1973 war, Egypt welcomed an increased American role in the region.

The United States took advantage of the opportunity to limit Soviet influence in a vital area by restraining and pressuring the Israelis. In addition, the growing American dependence upon Middle Eastern oil imports and the growing economic and political power of the Arab oil-producing countries (particularly Saudi Arabia) highlighted the divergence of interests between Israel and its major supporter, the United States. The issues of dispute between the two had been obscured in the years of bipolarity and before the Organization of Petroleum Exporting Countries (OPEC) became an effective force. Those differences had limited relevance as long as the Arabs refused to make peace and as long as Israel managed to carry the military burden without considerable support. Yet both conditions changed after 1973 (Safran, 1978:424; Sicherman, 1980:381-94; Inbar, 1984). First, the Arabs seemed to become, at least verbally, more conciliatory toward Israel. Egypt even signed a peace treaty with Israel in 1979. Second, Israel's security has become a much greater political and economic burden for the United States. Third, the United States has in the meantime become isolated in its support for Israel. Its European allies, considerably more dependent upon Arab oil, have made it increasingly clear that their Middle East position differs from the American one (Shimoni, 1981:92-107; Sicherman, 1980:845-57).

In the Middle East, as in other regional systems, the reduction in the bipolar dimension has placed the outcast in an uncomfortable position. Moreover, in spite of the fact that Israel's ally, the United States, seems to have become more influential in the region, it is a considerably weakened United States. The overthrow of the Shah (a reliable American ally in an important strategic area) made Iranian oil less secure to the West and forced the United States to become increasingly dependent upon the uninterrupted flow of Arab oil.

**Growth and Effectiveness of Third World States**
The emergence of the outcast state in the 1970s is connected to another systemic change—the increased cooperation and effectiveness of the Third World countries' coalition. The emergence of a stronger Third World bloc has been detrimental to outcast states, since they cannot easily become members of it. The Arabs' greater leverage in world politics is due to membership in this coalition. The Arabs, those sub-Sahara African nations who are members, and the PRC and North

Korea (which occasionally participate in these forums) all use the increased power of the Third World in their politicide drive against regional adversaries.

The loosening of the bipolar (East-West) structure in world politics strengthened the South-North (rather South-North West) cleavage which made the nonaligned (neutralist) nations and the Third World countries gradually more interchangeable and overlapping (Kimche, 1973; Mates, 1972; Ajami, 1980; Willets, 1978; Korany, 1976; Horowitz, 1966; Worsely, 1967; Miller, 1966).

The neutralist movement, initially consisting of Afro-Asian nations, regained momentum at the end of the 1960s because of growing radicalization in many parts of the globe. The nonaligned bloc also gained new converts in Latin America, in addition to Cuba, with the establishment of radical nationalist regimes, such as those in Peru and Panama in the late 1960s and Guyana and Jamaica in the 1970s. The Bandung Nonaligned Conference in 1955 was attended by twenty-nine states, the 1961 Belgrade Summit by twenty-five members plus three states with observer status. For the 1964 Cairo Summit the figures were forty-seven nations and ten observers. For the 1970 Lusaka Conference, the figures were fifty-seven and eleven, respectively, while the Algiers Summit in 1973 was attended by seventy-five states, eight observers and six liberation movements, all from Africa, Asia and Latin America (Yugoslavia being the only European participant). This trend of growth continued. The 1976 Colombo Summit was attended by eighty-five members, the 1979 Havana Summit by ninety-four members and the 1983 New Delhi Summit by ninety-six members.

The desire of some elites in the Third World to achieve equality of status and to project an image of power in world affairs led to the creation of regional and functional organizations (Nye, 1973:155). Third World countries have learned to coordinate their efforts in some issue areas, resulting in a new tricontinental loose coalition designed to pursue mutual political and economic interests. Third World economic demands were initially articulated at the first U.N. Conference for Trade and Development (UNCTAD) at Geneva in 1964. Those demands crystallized at the second UNCTAD at New Delhi in 1968 and culminated in a call for a new international economic order at the U.N. General Assembly in 1974.

Since the 1970 Lusaka Summit, this tricontinental loose coalition of nonaligned nations has begun to develop features of a formal institution. It holds regular meetings and elects an official spokesman, usually the leader of the summit meeting's host country, who has increasingly been endowed with administrative functions. It has set up a permanent executive committee (the Coordination Bureau) and formed a U.N. caucus group at the United Nations to coordinate Third World activities there (Willets, 1978:36-46).

The United Nations and its affiliates have proved to be a particularly effective forum for the Third World, which enjoys majority status there. Third World countries have used the United Nations to air grievances and legitimize demands by passing resolutions favorable to them. (This is, of course, not different from the way the United States used the United Nations in an earlier period when it could muster a majority.)

Third World activity is primarily directed against the white, capitalist, economically developed West, rather than the Eastern Communist bloc (Moynihan, 1975:31-44; Ajami, 1980:374-77; LeoGrande, 1980:33-52). The West, and primarily the United States, has continuously been attacked as neocolonialist and imperialist. Yet, in spite of Soviet verbal support for Third World demands, the Soviet position on North-South issues is ambiguous and the Soviet Union is hesitant to endorse programs that do not best serve its own interests (Gati, 1980:241-70). In effect, Third World countries took upon themselves the task of a moral entrepreneur (Becker, 1963:147). The egalitarian emphasis serves, of course, to dilute the distinction between states based on power calculations. Third World ideological rhetoric is basically an articulation of demands for redistribution of power and wealth, which is not very different from traditional international power politics (Tucker, 1975:39). Egalitarian ideology played a similar role in the breakdown of the concert system in Europe, particularly after 1890 (Rothstein, 1968). Ideology in this study is not perceived in a strict Marxist sense, which suggests that the role of ideas is only in veiling and justifying concrete group interests; ideology also means the values of the environment (internal and external) to which a country's elite responds (Geertz, 1964:47-76).

The Soviet Union and the Communist states support most Third World demands; this enhances communist influence in the Third World. Fulfillment of these demands, directed mainly at the North West, would also change the power relations in the international system and result in a further weakening of the West.

Interestingly, the West has displayed "understanding" for those demands. This sensitivity is based, to some extent, on feelings of guilt toward the underdeveloped nations, feelings reinforced by political and economic interests (Bauer, 1976:31-38). For example, Whitlam's

Australian Labor government (December 1972-November 1975) regularly voted with the Third World majority at the United Nations, or abstained. This was due to ideological preferences, as well as to an alliance with raw material exporters (Harries, 1975:1091). In addition, this "understanding" reflects the stronger bargaining position of some Third World actors; the West is not indifferent to important strategic locations, access to raw materials and markets or to investment opportunities (Bergsten, 1973:102-24).

Outcast states identified with the West have been at a particular disadvantage as a result of the greater leverage of Third World states and an unclear and inconsistent perceptual world map of Third World leaders and Third World Western sympathizers.

The Third World's condemnation of its adversaries has had a high priority in the United Nations; agreement on declaratory resolutions is easier than cooperation on more tangible issues where interests are not always mutual or complementary. Africans, for example, support anti-Israel resolutions. The Arab states' ascendancy in the Third World is obviously connected with their growing economic power (oil) and petrodollars. In addition to their economic might and numbers (twenty-two), the Arabs' Islamic identity (numerous Afro-Asian non-Arab countries are predominantly Muslim) has made Israel more vulnerable at the multilateral level. The Islamic revival further increased Israel's isolation (Lewis, 1976:33-49). Similarly, South Africa's isolation is, as mentioned, related to the emergence of independent black nations. The Communist countries reinforce the Third World in ostracizing the outcasts. Growing Chinese activity in Third World countries damaged Taiwan, and its animosity toward South Korea helped North Korea in its campaign against Seoul. Opponents of South Africa and Israel receive not only political support but military and economic aid from communist sources. Two of the outcasts, Taiwan and South Korea, face communist enemies, apart from communist propaganda.

Anti-Israeli propaganda, Arab and communist, gradually found a more receptive audience in the Third World. Arab successes in Third World countries were quite disappointing for Israel, which had initially (until 1973) succeeded in cultivating excellent relations with many of the Third World states. These bilateral relations had paid off initially at the multilateral level, too, reflected in the fact that the resolutions of international organizations and forums in the 1950s and most of the 1960s were not anti-Israeli or were only slightly unfavorable to the Jewish state.

Yet the emergence of an increasingly allied and institutionalized Third World, its radicalization and the Arab ascendancy in it gradually altered Third World countries' voting patterns on Middle East issues (Curtis and Gitelson, 1976:147-81; 182-99; 270-360). The perceptual map of Third World leaders (and others in the world) began to change after the 1967 war. First, Israel's stunning victory over three Arab enemies destroyed its image as an underdog. Israel, the "top dog" (victor), was separated from the Third World camp because Third World countries see themselves as the world's underdogs. Similarly, many circles in the West, as well as elsewhere, were incapable of showing support for a self-reliant and successful Israel. Humanitarians and social reformers seem to direct their concerns primarily to people who can be classified as helpless victims of causes and conditions beyond their control. The Indian and the Levantine communities in Africa and the Chinese in Southeast Asia are examples of persecuted minorities that evoke no sympathies (Bauer, 1976:161-62). Israel (the Jews), like Taiwan and to some extent South Korea, is "too successful" in facing political hostility.

Second, Israel's retention of territories conquered in war created apprehensions in the world community because of the general unpopularity of territorial adjustments for strategic purposes (since World War I) except on the grounds of self-determination (Rothstein, 1968:75; Kedourie, 1980). Self-determination is ignored, however, when it is in conflict with the strategic interests of some countries. The Baltic peoples are one obvious example. Palmerston (1954) once noted: "Great powers like Russia may persevere in wrongdoing and other states may not like the effort necessary for compelling it to take the right course. But no such impunity in wrongdoing is possessed by a small and weak state" (Taylor, 1954:147). The African countries were particularly sensitive to the issue of territorial integrity (Gitelson, 1976). Israeli reluctance to withdraw from occupied territories without an acceptable Arab quid pro quo provided good ammunition for Arab charges of Israeli expansionism. International attention has focused on territories Israel retains, rather than on the territory it has yielded. There was no amelioration in Israel's international status following the concessions in the 1975 Sinai 2 agreement. Even the renunciation of the entire Sinai in exchange for a peace treaty with Egypt did not change the role of Israel as an outcast country.

The third factor leading to Israel's political difficulties was the demand of the resurgent Palestinian national movement for self-determination. Those one-third of the Palestinians who have lived as refugees and another third who have lived under Israeli occupation found, not surprisingly, a sympathetic audience. Arabs presented the Jews' immigration to their homeland as one of white European colonizers exploiting, discriminating, and worst of all, uprooting native Asians. Reinforced by Soviet propaganda, which emphasized Israeli relations with South Africa and its links with the West, the effort seemed to be effective.

Fourth, the socioeconomic changes in Israel reinforce its identity as a Western island in an area of developing nations.

Fifth, the growing bipolarity in the Arab-Israeli core area of the Middle East, while the world became less bipolar, made Israel's pro-Western stance more objectionable. It is noteworthy that the Anglo-French-Israeli attack on Egypt in 1956, which could have "confirmed" the Israeli link to "imperialism," did not prevent the establishment of good relations with Afro-Asian nations in the following years. This is further indication that Israel's isolation is due to a particular international constellation, rather than to its deeds. Nevertheless, Israel did not attempt to disassociate itself from the United States and even savored the notion of being an American ally. For example, in the September 1970 Jordanian crisis, it willingly acted as such and emphasized this aspect. Since 1973, Israel has desired to play the role of American agent in the region (Rabin, 1979:313-15). Prime Minister Begin, more than labor leaders, enjoyed pointing out frequently that Israel is a loyal and valuable American ally.

The changing image of Israel, of course, only partially explains its position. National images should be regarded not only as causative, but also as symptomatic (Buchanan and Cantrill, 1953:57). Success in propaganda in world politics cannot be separated from successful use of other dimensions of power (Carr, 1939:26). The Arabs' oil wealth and their growing leverage in the changing international constellation gradually put Israel in a very unfavorable position.

## ISRAEL'S DETERIORATING INTERNATIONAL POSITION

The isolation of Israel became evident in the 1970s. Yet the process had started a decade earlier. As early as the 1960s, Third World countries like Burma (1962), Tanzania (1965) and Congo, Brazzaville (1966) had dispensed with Israeli aid. Following the 1967 war, all communist countries, with the exception of Romania, severed diplomatic relations with Israel. Ceylon suspended relations with Israel in June 1970 after the radical Mrs. Bandaranaike came to power. After 1970, African support for the Arab cause became significantly greater. Three factors may have contributed to the change of attitude: (1) the West's decreasing political interest in Africa, reflected in lessened financial aid; (2) the increasing flow of petrodollars, especially to countries with significant Muslim population; and (3) the growing radicalization in Africa (Gitelson, 1976:178-79). Indeed, in 1972, Chad and Mali (both of which have a large Muslim population), Niger and Congo, Brazzaville (both radical) severed diplomatic relations with Israel. They were joined, unexpectedly, by Amin's Uganda (1972). Burundi followed the trend in May 1973. The Algiers Summit of nonaligned nations (September 1973) adopted a greater number of resolutions against Israel than had similar forums in the past. Israel was branded colonialist and racist, together with South Africa, Rhodesia and Portugal. Moreover, the conference called for a diplomatic, economic, cultural and transportation boycott of Israel. As a result of the summit, Cuba and Togo immediately broke relations with Israel.

The October 1973 war was the catalyst for twenty-one additional African states (including Ethiopia, its informal regional ally) to sever diplomatic ties with Israel. This war "demonstrated" Israeli dependence on the "imperialist" United States. Another link with imperialism and colonialism was the Portuguese (at that time colonialist) provision of a fueling base in the Azores for the American airlift.

The next year, 1974, was not any better for Israel. The United Nations awarded Israel's arch-enemy, the PLO, observer status and its leader Arafat was welcomed by the General Assembly as a head of state (in violation of U.N. protocol). Israel was expelled in November 1974 from its regional UNESCO (United Nations Educational, Scientific, and Cultural Organization) section and the Arabs continued their efforts to oust Israel from other international organizations. In March 1974, radical Guyana joined the trend by severing its relations with Israel; it was followed by Cambodia and the Maldive Islands in 1975 and Laos and Mauritius in 1976.

In 1979, Iran, after the Islamic revolution, ended many years of fruitful cooperation with Israel by cutting relations with the "Zionist entity," and became one of the most vocal and generous supporters of the PLO. The Iranian Islamic fervor amplified the religio-cultural dimensions of the politicide campaign against Israel. The call for Jihad, a holy war, against the Jews—the infidels—not emphasized for some time in Arab capitals as concrete demands of Israel were stressed, became again a popular slogan. Further, the policy change of Iran, an important regional actor, increased Israel's regional isolation and damaged its "periphery doctrine," which stressed the importance of

32

cordial relations with those non-Arab states at the periphery of the Middle East—Ethiopia, Iran and Turkey. The Turkish government, under pressure from Muslim militants to sever its relations with Israel, has limited its athletic and cultural ties with Israel and in March 1981 lowered its diplomatic representation there.

The United Nations and its affiliated bodies have been the setting for most anti-Israel resolutions. The worst of these, from Israel's point of view, was the November 1975 U.N. General Assembly resolution branding Zionism as racism. In spite of heavy American lobbying against it, seventy-two countries voted in favor of the resolution, thirty-five opposed it and thirty-two abstained. The fact that among those voting to call Israel and its national revival movement "racist" were governments which themselves had racist policies of the worst, murderous sort (i.e., Sudan, Uganda) suggests that the label may bear no relevance to fact; nonetheless, the label may be effective. This resolution demonstrated the decreasing international legitimacy of the Jewish state even more profoundly than had the severance of diplomatic ties.

In December 1979 the United Nations again denounced Zionism as a form of racism. This time, the deterioration in Israel's international status was strikingly evident. Only three countries, the United States, Canada and Australia, opposed the resolution. No West European, Latin American or African state voted with Israel. An overwhelming 111 nations voted in favor of the resolution; only twenty-six abstained. Moreover, the 1979 resolution did not arouse the indignation of the free public as the 1975 anti-Zionist resolution had (that indignation had been one of the reasons the resolution was not resubmitted earlier).

Furthermore, the United Nations and its members seemed unaffected by the Egyptian-Israeli peace treaty, a tremendous step toward changing the nature of the regional conflict and opening the way for Israel's exit from outcast status. As a result of Arab prodding, the OAU heads of state meeting in Nairobi (June 1981) even condemned the Camp David accords. The United Nations refused to lend its tutelage to the peacekeeping force designed to supervise the implementation of the demilitarization clauses of the peace treaty. The United States also had difficulty recruiting foreign contingents to the multinational force it sponsored to perform the supervision task in Sinai.

Further deterioration occurred in August 1980, when U.N. members were called upon to move what embassies there were out of Jerusalem. Subsequently, all Latin American countries, as well as Israel's longtime supporter, the Netherlands, decided to move their embassies to Tel-Aviv. Their actions seriously set back Israel's efforts to gain international recognition of Jerusalem as its capital. This U.N. Security Council resolution was triggered by the passage of the Jerusalem Law in the Knesset, which was a formal reiteration that all of Jerusalem was Israel's capital. This critical reaction, when Israel in 1980 was quite isolated, is in contrast to Israel's decision to annex East Jerusalem following the Six-Day War in 1967 that evoked a rather mild opposition (Brecher, 1974:9-55). The difference in international reaction to similar measures is due primarily to changes in Israel's international environment.

Furthermore, U.S. abstention at the U.N. Security Council made possible for the first time the acceptance of a Security Council resolution that includes specific sanctions against Israel. This abstention was an indicator of the erosion in American support for Israel, already detectable since the "Reassessment" of 1975 when, following the failure of U.S. Secretary of State Henry Kissinger to bring about an Egyptian-Israeli agreement in March 1975, the Ford administration reassessed its Middle East policy. The administration blamed Israel for the breakdown of Kissinger's shuttle diplomacy and suspended negotiations with Israel over purchase of weapons and economic aid. The Carter administration's Spring 1978 attempt to tie the sale of planes to Saudi Arabia and Egypt to the delivery of promised aircraft to Israel, and John Connally's campaign for the Republican ticket for president in 1979 on an unprecedented anti-Israel platform, were additional signposts in the erosion process taking place in the United States. Even the Reagan administration, initially pro-Israel, eventually adopted unprecedented anti-Israel steps; on several occasions it suspended the delivery of weapons in violation of signed contracts.

In early 1981 the continuous Arab effort to oust Israel from the United Nations seemed to regain momentum. A resolution calling for Israel's expulsion passed for the first time at a meeting of the Foreign Ministers Third World Conference (New Delhi, February 1981). Similar attempts in such a forum had been unsuccessful in the past (Rivlin, 1979:41). The Arab League tried to expel Israel from the United Nations again in 1982 and 1983.

## EXIT FROM OUTCAST STATUS

Can Israel reverse this process of erosion? Under what circumstances is it possible for Israel or the other outcast states to rid themselves of outcast status as the PRC, Mauritania and Kuwait had accomplished earlier? Obviously, a change of policy of the rejected state is not necessarily sufficient to alter the character of the regional conflict. Neither Israeli withdrawal from occupied territories, improvement in the conditions of blacks in South Africa, nor an anti-American policy in Taiwan and South Korea will produce conciliation from the outcast states' opponents, so long as they cling to the politicide goal. Politicide was a necessary condition for qualification as an outcast state. Would elimination of this condition reverse the isolation process? The answer is no. Taiwan has not formally relinquished the goal of recapturing the mainland and bringing the PRC regime to an end. Its implicit acceptance of the "German formula" was a result of the PRC's success in breaking away from outcast status. The four current outcast states each faced a politicide drive long before acquiring ostracized status. Moreover, partial elimination of the politicide goal does not necessarily mean the end to outcast status. Even the Egyptian-Israeli peace treaty, which can be seen as the renunciation of politicide on the part of Israel's most powerful rival, has not ended Israel's isolation. Nevertheless, if the isolated state is to become a respectable member of the international community, only the regional acceptance of the outcast as an irrevocable fait accompli or the normative reconciliation to its existence can prevent the possibility of its emerging as an international outcast as a result of a new set of international circumstances in the future.

The normative reconciliation necessary for an end to politicide, inherently a lengthy regional psycho-political process, must occur in the societies of the outcasts' rivals and is to a great extent beyond the outcast's influence. It seems that the countries that have overcome isolation and politicide had a common characteristic: they shared cultural and national affinities with the people of the "enemy" state. Kuwaitis and Mauritanians were Arab just like Iraqis and Moroccans; German was spoken on both sides of the Iron Curtain. This affinity facilitated the psychological process of acceptance. In this respect, Taiwan and South Korea stand a better chance to escape the outcast condition than do Israel and South Africa.

Similarly, a change of rulers in the outcasts' rivals could be conducive to the exit from isolation, since new rulers are less bound by previous policies. The new German Chancellor Willy Brandt's Ostpolitik put an end to the German unification policies and the Hallstein Doctrine. The fall of Kassem in Iraq and the death of Mohammed V in Morocco enabled the new leaders of those countries to adopt a conciliatory policy toward their neighbors.

Creating the impression of unchallengeable permanency could also reverse the isolation process. The PRC's huge population and vast resources were instrumental in resisting attempts to isolate it. After the Communist regime consolidated its control over China, any attempt to challenge its legitimacy was doomed to failure. It became inconceivable that Taiwan, even with generous American support, could overthrow the Communist regime. On the other hand, the early Arab successes in the 1973 war destroyed Israel's invincible image and facilitated Arab, Muslim and international efforts to gain support for isolating Israel. Conversely, a drastic decrease in Arab military power as a result of inter-Arab wars, serious splits in the Arab coalition or a shift in national priorities could help Israel foster an image of invincibility. The Egyptian-Israeli treaty splits the Arab coalition and seriously hampers the chances for success of a future Arab military onslaught against Israel, should Egypt indeed stay out of such an engagement. The results of the treaty are still unclear, but the strategy of splitting the rival coalition has always been part of Israeli thinking. Such a strategy worked for Mauritania; Arab consensus favoring the Moroccan position, also supported by the Communist bloc, was shattered as Mauritania adopted a radical foreign policy and exploited the tensions between radicals and conservatives in the Arab camp.

The outcast's image of invincibility could be achieved also by the presence of a major extra-regional power. French troops stayed in Mauritania for five years after it gained independence; Morocco could not take any unilateral military measures against Mauritania in the face of its steadfast French support. Kuwait survived as a state in spite of Iraq's overwhelming military superiority, owing to the resolute support of British forces, subsequently replaced by an Arab League contingent, who forced Iraq to contemplate the high price to be paid for its irredentist claim. The permanent Soviet military presence in East Germany contributed to the Federal Republic's realization that the Hallstein Doctrine was unworkable. In contrast to the determined support of foreign powers for East Germany, Mauritania and Kuwait, American support for the four outcast states is problematic and cannot be taken for granted.

Global systemic changes could be an important factor in reducing isolation. The Soviet-American detente accelerated the acceptance of the post-World War II status quo, including a separate German Communist state. Similarly, changes in the two superpowers' balance of power in favor of the USSR accentuated the anomaly of the United States' anti-Peking policy. A redefinition of American interests in the outcasts' regions as a result of a more assertive American foreign policy could increase the political and military support to those countries and thus facilitate their exit from outcast status. Such a United States global policy, particularly if backed by greater economic and military power, could ease the situation of America's embattled allies. A more coordinated approach in this direction between the United States and its European allies toward the outcast's region could also ease the American burden in aiding an isolated state. As mentioned, however, the greater Western stake in the Middle East has caused difficulties for Israel. Therefore, a greater Western involvement in the outcast's region is beneficial to the international outcast only if it is perceived as positively enhancing the Western position in the area.

A widespread apprehension of Soviet imperialism, following the events in Afghanistan, Cambodia or in additional countries, could weaken or destroy nonaligned Third World and Soviet parallelism and enhance the international position of the United States and some of its anti-Soviet allies. Both developments—a more assertive Washington and a more feared Moscow—would contain benefits for the outcast states. Indeed, Africa's growing apprehension of the Soviet presence on their continent is one reason for greater cooperation with Israel on the part of pro-Western countries such as Zaire, Liberia, Togo and Gabon (*Maariv,* 20 August 1983; interviews with Israeli officials, Summer 1983). President Mobutu of Zaire even renewed his country's diplomatic relations with Israel in May 1982. Liberia followed Zaire's example in August 1983. The turmoil in Central America and the greater Communist-supported activities in that area similarly strengthened relations between Israel and Central American countries. Costa Rica and El Salvador even decided in 1983 to move their embassies back to Jerusalem.

South Korea has also benefited from Japan's perception of the Soviet Union as a potential threat. Japan has increased its own defense spending and also has agreed to provide South Korea with $4 billion in economic aid over a five-year period, directly affecting the military strength of that country (Maynes, 1983:27).

Similarly, a reduction in the South-North West tensions could lead to a greater recognition of the positive role the outcast states can play as agents of modernization in their regions and elsewhere. Israel and Taiwan, in particular, have already contributed to the development of many Third World countries through elaborate foreign assistance programs.

Changes in the international political economy as a result of the discovery of substantial oil reserves in the West, or the development of cheap energy substitutes, could help Israel eventually exit from outcast status. Food shortages on a global scale could lead to a Western food cartel (United States, Canada, Australia); such a scenario could again strengthen the West and the outcast states allied with it.

Systemic conditions are indeed more important to exiting from outcast status than regional developments. Israel's outcast status has not decreased as a result of the 1979 Egyptian-Israeli peace treaty. Although the politicide campaign against Israel by other Arab countries continues, its outcast condition remains, in spite of a regional detente, as a result of Egypt's substantially reduced regional and international status in the 1970s. In the 1960s, under the charismatic leadership of Nasser, Egypt enjoyed great international prestige as one of the Third World's leading countries, and held the primary position in the Arab world. But Egypt's defeat in 1967, the death of Nasser in 1970 and the ascendance of Arab oil-producing nations, particularly Saudi Arabia, ended Egypt's hegemony in the Arab world and curtailed its international influence.

Israel's Arab neighbors have in the past usually followed Egypt's leadership; Egypt's step toward reconciliation with Israel might have led the Arab world to give up politicide as a historic and moral imperative and to accept Israel. Yet what has actually happened in the five years since Sadat's historic visit to Jerusalem (November 1977) is, rather, increased isolation of *Egypt*. Isolation by association with an outcast reflects Egypt's decline as an international actor. Yet this isolation is designed to pressure Egypt to change its policy and is not a desire to dissolve the Egyptian state. Egypt's pro-Western turn, coupled with the animosity of the Arab confrontation states, undermined its position in the Third World countries and exposed Egypt to accusations of being an ally of the neocolonialist and imperialist forces. Sadat refrained from participation in the 1979 OAU Summit and in the 1980 Havana Nonaligned Summit to spare himself the embarrassment of a cool reception. The Arab confrontation states even attempted to oust Egypt, one of the founders of the nonaligned movement, from the nonaligned bloc at the Colombo preparatory meeting in June 1979. The Havana Summit suspended Egypt's membership in the nonaligned movement for eighteen months, threatening Egypt with expulsion from the movement unless it changed its foreign policy. Even West European countries initially showed coolness toward the Egyptian-Israeli treaty, and Japan refused to host an official visit of Sadat (*Maariv*, 16 October 1979). The potentially lucrative air route between Cairo and Tel-Aviv did not appeal to American or European carriers because of fears of

Arab boycotts and terrorist hijackings (*Newsweek,* 2 July 1978). Arab politics, changing Arab threat perceptions and a militarily and economically stronger Egypt combined to make Cairo once again a leading regional actor. Resumption of Egyptian-Sudanese diplomatic relations in May 1981, severed by Sudan—and all other Arab countries except Oman and Somalia—in protest of the peace treaty with Israel, was possibly the beginning of such a process. As could be expected from the analysis above, the change of rulers after Sadat's assassination (October 1981), as well as the threat perceived by many Arab countries following the expulsion of the Iraqi forces from Iran, led to closer Arab relations with Egypt. In January 1984 the Casablanca Islamic Conference even decided to readmit Egypt to this forum. It is noteworthy that, in the post-Sadat era, Egypt's foreign policy again emphasizes nonalignment, in contrast to the pro-American orientation of Sadat (Boutros-Ghali, 1982). Mubarak, Sadat's successor, has also lowered considerably the profile of Egypt's relations with Israel. Furthermore, according to some reports (*Maariv,* 27 January 1984), Mubarak intends to distance himself from the Camp David accords—the basis of the peace treaty with Israel. In spite of these changes, Egypt has not yet formally reconciled with the Arab world. Only Jordan renewed its diplomatic relations with Egypt in December 1984. If Egypt regains its position in the Arab world not at the expense of its treaty with Israel, this would help Israel in its quest for recognition in the Arab world.

In the meantime, the peace treaty with Egypt did not alleviate Israel's international isolation. This indicates the importance of systemic factors in Israel's current misfortune. The international difficulties of Egypt as a result of its association with Israel demonstrate as well the relevance of systemic constraints on relations with outcast states.

## CONCLUSION

Outcast states are states subject to imposed isolation and to a politicide campaign. Their opponents conduct an international campaign challenging the legitimacy of the outcast's existence. The outcasts are relatively small countries identified as pro-Western in conflict with a non-Western regional power. Belonging to the Western camp as a formal or an informal ally did not prevent their isolation and does not assure the outcasts security because of the ambiguity surrounding the American commitment to non-European regions. The outcasts' link to the West is not part of their definition, but part of their predicament; their situation is difficult not only because they are linked to the West but also because this link seems to be increasingly tenuous.

The outcast state phenomenon stems from the globalization of regional politics. Israel, like the other outcast states, has acquired that status primarily because of changes in the international system. The growing multipolarity in world affairs and the weakening of the American position enhanced the Third World coalition, which became increasingly coordinated and powerful. The outcast states' adversaries have succeeded in mobilizing the Third World and the Communist camp to delegitimize and weaken their rivals. Their success in the Third World has also served as an indirect pressure on the West to adopt anti-outcast policies. Israel, in particular, has been at a disadvantage, since its opponents have gained considerable leverage in an oil-thirsty world. The Arab states, members of the Third World movement, have been consequently more successful in pressing their cause as dependence on Middle East oil increased. Outcast states obviously cannot influence global developments; this limits the range of strategies available to oppose the politicide campaign against them. The next chapter deals with strategies the isolated states can adopt.

# 3

## STRATEGIES

This chapter discusses strategies that make sense for Israel and the other outcast states in order to prevent the total isolation that may lead to their destruction. Two factors must be taken into consideration when devising strategies for the ostracized states of the 1970s. The first, discussed in chapter 2, is the unfriendly international environment. Indeed, any discussion of a small state's foreign policy should start by identifying its international environment, since the environmental variables are more important for it than for a superpower (Bjöl, 1971:34). The second factor, discussed here, is the strategy of the outcasts' opponents. One characteristic of strategy is the interdependence on other actors (conflictual and/or cooperative) (Schelling, 1970:5). The strategy of the outcast state's rivals, defined here as the indirect strategy, and its consequences, are analyzed first. Subsequently, four strategies for the outcast states are discussed: (a) entrenchment, (b) accommodation, (c) realignment, and (d) a mixed strategy. These strategies are analytical options within a particular historic context and constitute possible responses to the strategy of the outcast state's opponents. These strategies are not exclusive, however, to outcast states.

### STRATEGY FOR THE OUTCASTS' OPPONENTS

This strategy can be characterized as indirect strategy. The essential feature of an indirect strategy is its emphasis on methods other than the direct use of military means to achieve victory (Beaufre, 1970:108). The concept should not be confused with the strategic concept of "indirect approach," which refers to military maneuver; the indirect strategy falls into the category of "grand strategy."

The Arab states, the PRC, North Korea and the sub-Sahara African nations could "solve" their respective problems if Israel, Taiwan, South Korea and South Africa could be respectively defeated on the battlefield and occupied. The enemies of the international outcasts do not presently have the military resources to accomplish such a solution, however, and seek to obtain their goals via political action at the multilateral level (the exterior maneuver) rather than at the regional level (the interior maneuver) (Beaufre, 1970). The indirect strategy attempts to sever the outcast's political, economic and military links to the international community. Opponents attempt to shape conditions far beyond their national boundaries in a strategy whose objective Wolfers (1963:67-80) once called "milieu goals." Moreover, it tries to make the intended outcast an unacceptably heavy burden (political, economic and military) for the West and primarily for the United States, the outcast's major ally. The primary objective of the indirect strategy is to break or weaken the outcast's vital link to the United States. Arab leaders view U.S. support of Israel crucial to its existence. Already at the first Arab Summit (January 1964) Nasser stated that military action against Israel can take place only after Israel had been isolated diplomatically (Gilboa, 1969:38). U.S. military presence in South Korea seems to be very important in deterring an invasion. Similarly, the abrogation of the U.S.-Taiwan defense treaty facilitates the realization of a military solution should Communist China become strong enough militarily for such a campaign. Indeed, if successful in the indirect strategy, it becomes easier to achieve the ultimate goal—politicide.

Apart from the marginality of the outcast state and the narrowing of U.S. interests in the outcast, the bilateral relationship is in itself problematic. The relationship of the extra-regional power, the United States to Israel, to Taiwan, to South Korea and to some extent to South Africa, can be regarded as a patron-client arrangement. This relationship is characterized by a reciprocal but asymmetrical flow of benefits and the absence of coercion on the part of the patron state in spite of the vast differences in resources, capabilities and material needs (Knorr, 1975:25-26). This relationship between the extra-regional power and its local ally is inherently unstable and unsatisfactory (Vital, 1971:25-26; Rothstein: 1968, 57-58, 62). The local power is consulted by its larger ally only on those matters where it can make a contribution (as the big power sees it), and tends to suspect its larger ally of seeking a regional agreement at its expense (Shurke, 1973:513). The unequal partners in the alliance also have conflicting perspectives. The United States, for example, sees things from a global perspective, tending sometimes toward global parochialism (a global perspective that loses information and details of particular regions) (Rudolph and Rudolph, 1975), while the outcast's perspective is essentially regional. Furthermore, the outcast, being a small state, has limited margins of security, while the United States is accustomed to larger ones. There is also an inevitable tension between U.S. actions to further its presence in the region and actions to protect its client, the outcast, which cannot be allowed to fall.

Opponents of outcast states usually initiate political action in order to increase tensions between the outcast and its Western supporters, but military means characteristic of the regional relations are not excluded (for example, Israel, and to a lesser extent, South Africa, face terrorist attacks). Rivals of the outcast states may also initiate a war of attrition (a limited use of force designed to heighten tension and with no immediate intention of gaining territory), or fight limited wars (Heikal, 1976:414-26; Fairbanks, 1976:164-226). For example, the PRC bombarded Quemoy Island in 1954 to create tensions that might split the United States from the nationalist government or lead to United States withdrawal (Barnett, 1974:252-53). Rivals may also use violence to weaken the outcast's national power, i.e., to undermine its economy, its morale and, if possible, its political institutions; or to achieve limited regional goals such as recovery of lost land in the Middle East or improvement in the conditions of blacks in South Africa.

This violence is also closely connected with the exterior maneuver (the extra-regional objective). A terror campaign against Israeli targets is designed to maximize publicity for the conflict. This violence at the regional level attracts worldwide attention and crystallizes support for "solving" the problem. The solution advocated by most countries, however, is not likely to be acceptable to the outcast state.

Military exchanges can also escalate into a superpower confrontation, an undesirable development in the opinion of the superpowers. The United States, a status quo power, is particularly intent on preventing eruptions of violence in regional conflicts that could draw it into a greater level of involvement and become politically and economically costly. The military forces of Israel, Taiwan and the Republic of Korea are largely equipped and financed by the United States; any military action there taxes U.S. economic resources. Often the bill for regional military exchanges is sent to Washington; for example, the United States had to increase considerably the financial assistance to Israel following the 1973 Yom Kippur War.

Internationalization of regional conflict benefits, to some extent, the outcast states as well. They have benefited from the bipolar dimension; so long as the United States is dedicated to policies of global involvement, a small ally is assured of some U.S. support (Keohane, 1971:163). Internationalization of the conflict coupled with some U.S. cooperation may be enough to secure for the outcast continuing U.S.

support, though its adequacy may be debatable. A reduction of global tensions or a policy of greater accommodation on the part of the United States toward its international competitors could cause American support to be less forthcoming in the future.

At the same time, internationalization of conflict exacerbates relations within the region. Moreover, it places the outcast in confrontation with a superpower (Taiwan, which happens to oppose an enemy of one superpower and continues to receive limited support from the other, is the exception). In addition, it constrains the outcast's freedom of action since global developments have to be taken into consideration. These same global restraints provide its rivals with greater freedom of action and international support. The opening of hostilities is, for example, politically more costly for the outcast than for its opponents. Furthermore, the advertised alliance with the United States damages its international image with Communist and Third World governments.

Outcast states, including Israel, do not have the option of localizing conflict; their regional relationships are enmeshed in superpower interests, and these global linkages are consciously exploited by their regional enemies. Political actions at the global level are supplemented and/or complemented by violence on the local level against the outcast state to weaken it.

The attempt to undermine the outcast's support from its extra-regional ally is, however, to agree to a lengthy process. The indirect strategy presumes a protracted struggle that requires great moral or ideological commitment, as in revolutionary guerrilla warfare, as well as time (Beaufre, 1970:116-17). The enemies of outcast states have similarly developed ideological structures to support such a continuous conflict, claiming that history is on their side, an idea that enhances their psychological preparedness for protracted conflict. Arabs view their campaign against Israel as the continuation of the historic Arab struggle against Western imperialism. Sub-Sahara Africa similarly regards the decolonization process as destined to reach Southern Africa in order to end the white supremacy in the sub-Sahara African continent. The struggle of the PRC and North Korea is rooted in Marxist as well as nationalist fervor.

**Consequences of the Exterior Maneuver**

A campaign against the outcast extends beyond the geographic area of the conflict in order to isolate the outcast state in the international arena. The obvious question is to what extent does isolation really threaten the national security of the international outcast?

Severance of diplomatic relations, accompanied by a statement of reproach, or even withdrawal of recognition, may in the short run be of little consequence since the value of diplomatic relations with most countries, especially Third World countries, is often marginal. Israel continues to trade with sub-Sahara African or Communist countries in spite of the absence of diplomatic relations. Mutual interests also facilitate continuous or occasional cooperation. Kenya seems to have cooperated with Israel in the Entebbe raid (July 1976) against its eccentric neighbor, Uganda, then led by Idi Amin. Ethiopia, in spite of a radical turn and its subsequent anti-Israeli stand, continues to share with Israel an interest in preventing the Red Sea from becoming an Arab lake. South Africa, too, has continuously traded with hostile countries of the continent to their mutual benefit. In spite of some inconveniences, Taiwan continues to engage in profitable economic relations, as well as cultural interaction, with most countries that have withdrawn official recognition.

One goal of isolating the outcast is to psychologically wear out its people. The morale of a people is an important factor in the military power of any state (Knorr, 1956:43; Vital, 1967:81). The dedication of a society and its willingness to make sacrifices are crucial for sustaining the defense effort (Howard, 1982). A key question, then, is to what extent have the changing international conditions and pressures applied on the outcast states weakened the motivation of their people to withstand the long conflict?

On the one hand, the threat of isolation can help handicapped people be brave and heroic in the face of challenge. People would make a virtue of isolation. Martyrdom has always had appeal. The effort to draw strength from one's weakness has been defined by psychologists as a compensatory mechanism (Wood, 1963:215). On the other hand, psychological and material hardships may break the spirit of a society.

Morale is difficult to measure. Moreover, even when measured, no clear causal relationship can be established, although polls measuring the level of confidence in the leadership can be an indicator. Satisfaction with the Israeli government in the post-1973 period oscillated considerably. In South Africa, Vorster's party gained an electoral victory in 1977, but it is not clear exactly how the victory was related to the morale of the "white tribe."

The trend of emigration from a country may also serve as an indicator of morale (Hirschman, 1970). Israel and South Africa are making efforts to increase their Jewish and white populations, respectively, through immigration. Emigration is a setback to a governmental policy and reflects lack of faith in the future of a country, weariness from living with an endless conflict, etc. South Africa experienced in 1977, for the first time, a net loss of white population, when emigration exceeded immigration. In Israel the growing numbers of emigrants for several years following the October 1973 war have not been matched by higher levels of immigration. Although dissatisfaction with the situation can be definitely detected, it is an exaggeration to conclude that national morale was sagging. Taiwan and South Korea seem less concerned by such a problem. Those countries may face, however, subversion from their Communist brethren across the border.

The influence of a hostile resolution to conflict by an international forum or the cumulative impact of international isolation upon the spirits of a people are not clear. Moreover, a nation's will is not necessarily broken by the impact of recurring wars. Jews and others have demonstrated a strong will to continue business as usual in spite of perennial violence. Outcast states seem less vulnerable to psychological pressure due to international isolation than their enemies would like to admit. Economic pressure seems, in fact, to affect national morale more than psychological pressure; as long as the outcast states can avoid a sharp decline in their standard of living, other hardships are probably manageable.

The PRC and North Korea believe, of course, that any capitalist society is susceptible to propaganda. Moreover, they hope that the working class will eventually develop class consciousness to facilitate the transition to a communist society. Sub-Sahara African countries also hope that South Africa's blacks will develop a more effective guerrilla warfare. In addition, there are hopes that the liberal voices in the white community will gain a greater number of supporters. Arabs try to exploit the Ashkenazi/Sephardi difference and radical groups appeal to the Israeli working class. In the past, attempts to use psychological warfare have not been successful in these countries.

If diplomatic isolation and withdrawal of recognition are of negligible importance in the short run, they are dangerous in another area. In the long run, the image of the international outcast may entrench itself in the international culture, the set of beliefs, norms and values engendered in diplomatic intercourse (Modelski, 1961:122; Holsti; 1974:373-74). The goal of politicide is explained as a need to respond to violations of international norms. Israel, for example, is accused of denying self-determination to the Palestinians, and of annexation by force—both acts contrary to systemic values. Most countries refuse to have diplomatic relations with the outcast states, however, primarily because of pragmatic reasons related to the international power constellations. For example, many African countries severed diplomatic ties with Israel only after threats and promises from rich Arab oil-producing nations (Gitelson, 1976:187-88). Similarly, policy makers in countries that withdrew recognition from Taiwan simply perceived gains would be greater than losses in such a diplomatic course.

Yet for the outcast, the danger is that such reality-oriented attitudes of many national elites, particularly in the West, may turn into symbolic beliefs, which are more persistent (Katz, 1965:354-90). For example, U.N. decisions could be normatively accepted rather than viewed as the output of inter-state bargaining. The Israeli case is a good example of conversion of reality-oriented attitudes to ideological reasoning. In 1967 Israel was viewed in the West as acting rightfully on the principle of self-defense. Gradually, as a result of systemic changes, its position on secure and recognized borders became less acceptable and now Israel is often accused of expansionism. The analogy of the Palestinian issue to the Sudeten Germans offers an even more striking example of such a conversion. In both cases, parts of enlightened Western public opinion gradually gave in, respectively, to growing Nazi and Arab power and consequently to their propaganda, and gradually came to view the Sudeten Germans and Palestinians as oppressed national groups deprived of their right to self-determination (Plaut, 1980:23-27). Similarly, as a result of China's ascendance in world politics, the Taiwanese refusal to be "reunited" could conceivably be viewed in the near future as an intransigent position on the part of a reactionary and illegal government, which constitutes a danger to regional peace.

Western elites and public opinion are influenced by the recurring negative attitudes toward the outcast that emanate from international bodies. If those attitudes are emulated, this will further weaken the outcast state's base of support in the West. The character of bilateral relations with a country is also influenced by the internationally assigned status of a national actor (Singer and Small, 1966:238). The deterioration of Western public opinion support for Israel and Taiwan is partly due to such an emulation. The politicide struggle of the outcasts' opponents, which precipitated isolation, may therefore gain not only acquiescence, but also normative approval.

Diplomatic isolation facilitates taking positive international actions against the outcast. The politicide struggle can escalate beyond the regional level to international condemnation, eviction from international forums, international economic sanctions and eventually internationally organized military intervention.

47

South Africa has experienced almost all rungs of this escalation ladder. It was first condemned and then expelled from international bodies. Subsequently, economic sanctions were imposed, followed by an arms embargo. Recently, a demand for international military intervention has also been voiced.

Unfavorable international resolutions can be lived with. A vote of condemnation at the U.N. Security Council, for example, is not a pleasant experience, but it can often be ignored. Indeed, Israel has ignored all U.N. resolutions concerning Jerusalem and has to a great extent developed a psychological immunity to U.N. resolutions. Daniel P. Moynihan, U.S. Ambassador to the U.N. (1975-1976), summed up Israeli attitudes: "They confined their responses to a narrow range between indifference to defiance" (Moynihan, 1978:266; see also Brecher, 1972:144, 159). South Africa seems to have adopted a similar disposition.

International economic sanctions, however, can hurt a country much more, and not only in the strict economic sense. The economy is an important variable in the ability of a state to marshal military power. Moreover, the weakest spot in a small power's defense line is probably the economic one (Vital, 1967:55). In the economy of a small or medium-size country, limited resources and limited local markets create a dependence upon foreign trade for exports as well as for imports. Countries whose greater part of their gross national product is connected to international trade, and whose contribution to global trade is easily replaceable, are particularly vulnerable to economic pressures (Marcy, 1963:269; Triffin, 1963:248-65). Israel, Taiwan and South Korea are in such a situation; South Africa is somewhat less vulnerable because of its immense natural riches. Moreover, outcast states have little ability to retaliate against economic warfare with similar measures. In this, South Africa is not an exception. In spite of its bountiful mineral reserves, it does not have enough concentration of any mineral, with the exception of chromium, to place it in a position similar to Arab oil producers. Chromium, however, is not of comparable economic importance. Therefore, no outcast has the ability to conduct economic warfare.

It is claimed, however, that collective economic sanctions tend to be ineffective. First, some states do not abide by the international resolutions for ideological and/or political reasons. Second, the cost of participating may be too high for some countries. Third, countries with free enterprise may find it difficult to stop illicit trading (Knorr, 1975:146-65; Friedman, 1980:48). In addition, economic pressures tend to affect a target state only after a good deal of time. This time lag may permit some sort of accommodation, especially if the sanctions are gradually applied. The economic sanctions initiated by the League of Nations against Italy, for example, or the more recent boycotts against Rhodesia or South Africa seemed to have little effect on the disputed politics of the mentioned countries. Boycotts seem to be employed by countries that feel the need to do something short of military action. A boycott also keeps the issue alive and makes the receiver of sanctions in some sense an outcast (Roberts, 1975:577-79).

Israel, for example, did not grant much significance to the Arab economic boycott until 1974. Yet following the October 1973 war, Israel became more sensitive to the actual and potential harm of the Arab boycott, according to Israel's former Deputy Director General for International Affairs and other senior economists in the Finance Ministry. In addition to their greater financial leverage following the oil crisis, Arabs controlled a great part of the oil production—a very important commodity in an oil-thirsty world. At that time, Israel's buying power also declined drastically relative to that of the Arabs.

As a result of the new Arab economic power and the greater efficiency of the Arab boycott, the Israeli economy was more affected than before. It is difficult to put a price on the harm done. Yet since the October 1973 war, two areas were clearly negatively influenced by the boycott—foreign investment and purchase of foreign know-how. Multinational companies tend to refrain from activity in Israel. An additional cost to the economy is the increased stockpiling Israel has to do because it fears supplies may be stopped. The Israeli export is not seriously harmed by the boycott, because it constitutes in most cases a small part of the world market and alternative buyers can be found, though occasionally with some difficulty. The availability of imports has generally not been reduced, but it often costs more when the boycott has to be bypassed. One particularly affected area is oil imports. Even Western countries like England and Norway refused to sell oil to Israel, even though the United States tried to convince the two countries to do so (*Maariv,* 13 April 1979). Norway finally agreed to oil transactions with Israel only at the end of 1983 when the oil glut forced it to find new clients (*Maariv,* 21 December 1983). Israel was fortunate to find in Mexico a willing oil supplier after Khomeini's Iran stopped oil deliveries to Israel.

Interestingly, weapons procurement is not affected by the boycott per se. Formally, the regulations of the boycott free Arab countries from any constraints when purchasing arms from firms doing business with Israel. Arab countries, following the example of Africa's struggle to stop arms sales to South Africa, have tried to impose an arms embargo on Israel through the United Nations. In 1978, Iraq initiated a U.N. General Assembly resolution to place an embargo on arms deliveries to Israel. The resolution was passed by seventy-two nations in favor and thirty opposing (*Jerusalem Post,* 11 December 1978). In the meantime, this resolution had no practical effect.

Israelis are acutely aware of the danger of economic isolation. They feared a sudden "avalanche effect" in submission of Western firms to the Arab boycott regulations. Israel, like the other outcasts, has a great stake in trade with the West, the outcasts' major trade partner and main source of outside investment. Moreover, only the West can supply credit for economic development and purchase of weapons. The West's support for economic sanctions is crucial for the successful economic isolation of the outcast state. Israel, therefore, made great efforts to fight the Arab boycott in the West in the post-1973 period by attempting to influence American and European legislative bodies to outlaw the secondary and the tertiary boycott. This campaign, started in 1974, has had various degrees of success. According to Israeli officials, Israel is still apprehensive about the efforts of the Arab boycott and growing Arab economic power.

The economic campaign against the ostracized state coupled with a normative acceptance of politicide can escalate to an internationally organized military intervention against the outcast state. What are the chances for such an intervention? Is it conceivable that Third World and/or Soviet allied countries may decide to send military troops to participate in military action against an outcast state?

A U.N. General Assembly resolution or one by a Third World forum in favor of an international force to operate against an outcast state or to place a blockade upon it is not a far-fetched scenario. The outcast status of a target state may facilitate the passing of such a resolution. The United Nations has already decided upon economic sanctions and an arms embargo against South Africa. The OAU repeatedly demanded to intensify "the liberation struggle" against the white regimes in Southern Africa. Terrorist groups from all over the world cooperate against Israel, and the violence may well escalate from terrorism to more intensive warfare. Arab contingents from countries not bordering Israel have participated in wars against Israel. In addition, Cuban, North Korean and, of course, Soviet military presence across the Israeli border has been often reported. The Soviet Union even actively participated in defending the Egyptian skies in 1970 and approaches a similar involvement in Syria since 1983.

50

An international military intervention (a modern crusade against an outcast) is a conceivable scenario, particularly if direct American support for the outcast is unlikely. Then the Soviet Union may decide to participate in a war against Israel or South Africa, for example. The costs of transportation for intervention have declined (Wohlstetter, 1968:242-55). The Soviet Union has already displayed the logistic capability for such a campaign—it ferried Moroccan troops to fight on the Golan Heights in 1973 and helped transport and equip thousands of Cubans to fight in Africa. Soviet air transport capability, tested by a massive airlift to the Middle East and Africa in October 1979, proved remarkable. Further, the Soviet navy is increasingly capable of mounting amphibious operations and to offer sea-based air support for inland operations (Zumwalt, 1980:419-510; Connell, 1980:129-48).

The likelihood of an international force being committed to fight against an outcast depends upon the creation of a community of interests among the regional enemies of the outcast and extra-regional powers. A passive American attitude also enhances the chances of intervention. Finally, military weakness, or lack of the outcast's resolution to fight, is an important element. The higher the probable price extracted of the international intervening force by the outcast, the less likely the force will be organized and deployed. In her study of small powers, Annette Baker Fox emphasizes that the willingness to fight has contributed to small power independence (Fox, 1957:42, 77).

There are now greater constraints on the use of military power, and its political utility has diminished (Knorr, 1966:Ch. 3). Yet the political price has not increased equally for all nations. The 1956 Anglo-French-Israeli invasion of Egypt was treated differently by Third World countries and the United Nations than the Soviet Union's military intervention in Hungary at the same time. More recently, South Africa's participation in 1976 in Angola's civil war was less tolerable in international forums than the participation of Cuban troops from across the ocean. Constraints on the use of force are greater on the United States and Western countries than on Third World countries (Knorr, 1977:5-27).

Obviously, Israel or the other outcast states cannot fight successfully against a large-scale international effort supported by the Soviet Union. U.S. support is needed to deter Soviet direct participation or massive involvement on the part of its satellites. Yet an outcast country can achieve a deterrent force against a limited international effort. In this case Western support is needed, too. The most crucial issue for the outcast states is weapons procurement. Presently, Israel, Taiwan, South

Korea and South Africa depend upon a supply of modern Western weapons. These countries are making efforts to achieve a greater level of self-sufficiency in this area, but it is very difficult, for technological and economic reasons, to build an indigenous industry capable of fully substituting for Western equipment.

Western and especially American assistance to the international outcast is a critical element in its security. The United States prevents the outcast from becoming completely isolated, where the economic and military consequences would be unbearable. For, as we have said, any reduction in the level of political, economic or military support, or in trade volume, can affect negatively the national security of the outcast state.

Termination of United States commitments—the goal of the indirect strategy—is one of the major fears of the outcast states (Podhoretz, 1976:23-31; Rom, 1979; Shamir, 1979; McBeath, 1977:18-26; Han, 1978:45-50; Barrat, 1976:147-68). Yet in spite of the United States' tendency to reduce its commitments abroad, the Vietnamese debacle could make the abandonment of an ally more difficult, especially if that ally does not need an American fighting contingent. The United States, if only to maintain its credibility as an ally, has some reason to support an embattled ally on the margins. What are the circumstances, however, which facilitate a disengagement from the troubled alliance with the outcast?

First, we should distinguish between an abrupt abandonment and a slow disengagement process (Deibel, 1978:17-35). The first possibility is rather unlikely. Withdrawing recognition, severance of diplomatic relations, a stoppage of economic assistance and an arms embargo are drastic measures, which any American administration may have difficulties in implementing at one time. Just the derecognition of Taiwan, which was preceded by a six-year PRC-American rapprochement and without an arms embargo or any other measures, evoked a stiff resistance in the U.S. Congress and in public opinion. Yet, almost four years later, in August 1982, the Reagan administration unexpectedly announced a long-term policy to gradually reduce its sales of arms to Taiwan. In the case of Israel, this process of slow desertion could take the form of a gradual reduction in the magnitude of economic support, a progressively less responsive weapons supply policy—qualitatively and quantitatively, a slow erosion in United States support at the United Nations and other international forums, and a lowering of the level of diplomatic representation.

What events could lead to such a disengagement? The continuation of the systemic trends discussed earlier, which initially brought about the emergence of the outcast state, could further strain the relations between the shunned state and the United States to the point of a deliberate American effort to terminate the relationship. Particularly, an intensification of the American isolationist predisposition and/or a growing pressure on the United States from the outcasts' opponents may speed such a process of relinquishment. Nuclearization of a regional subsystem, where the outcast state or one of its enemies acquires nuclear capability, could also make a superpower commitment less likely, since such an involvement could escalate to a nuclear superpower confrontation. Moreover, an international norm against nuclear proliferation has been established, although some claim that the nuclear taboo has been weakened by the Indian atomic explosion and the prospects of similar occurrences in Pakistan, Iraq or Brazil. But nuclear weapons in the hands of an outcast state might be judged differently.

The pace of deterioration in the bilateral relations between the outcast and the United States also depends on the outcast's foreign policy. Certain actions could provide a good pretext for disengagement. A first regional nuclear test by Israel or South Africa is an example of an "inadmissible" deed from Washington's point of view. An aggressive retaliatory policy against bordering countries on the part of Israel, South Africa or South Korea could become a catalyst for disengagement. For example, in response to Israeli military actions, the question whether Israel made a legitimate use of its American-supplied weapons has been raised often in recent years. Furthermore, Israel's incursion into Lebanon in March 1978 elicited American threats. The air raid on the Iraqi reactor (June 1981) and the June 1982 invasion of Lebanon even evoked American sanctions of unprecedented nature—suspensions of delivery of military equipment. Indeed, territorial conquests on the part of an outcast could trigger a gradual American breakaway. Disengagement is therefore facilitated in case the outcast can be credibly accused of raising regional tensions and of not showing a certain minimal cooperation with United States policies.

Gradual abandonment can take place also in case a regional agreement has been reached, even if only a formal "peace with honor" in the manner of the Vietnamese settlement. The Chinese tacit agreement to refrain from pleading for a military solution to the Taiwan problem is an example of such a scenario. In the Middle East, United Nations and other international guarantees to Israel's security could lead to a similar United States disengagement.

## STRATEGIES FOR THE OUTCAST STATE

The exterior maneuver of the indirect strategy is designed to weaken the link of the outcast to the West. Four strategies are available to the outcast states to cope with this predicament: entrenchment, accommodation, realignment and a mixed strategy. These strategies are logical options arrived at after considering the unfavorable international circumstances of the 1970s, the actions of the opponents of the outcasts in the international arena and the problematic relationship of the isolated state with its major supporter—the United States. The likelihood of a change in the global situation is considered to be small in the short run, that is five to ten years. Similarly, the goal of politicide is not likely to be relinquished in the near future by the outcasts' opponents, although the intensity of pursuing it may vary. Even Egypt, in spite of its peace treaty with Israel, has not ceased its anti-Israeli diplomatic activity. For example, its U.N. delegation often votes in favor of anti-Israeli resolutions.

When measuring the merits of each strategy and its chances of being adopted by Israel or the other ostracized countries, several criteria have to be taken into consideration: (a) the extent to which the strategy can reduce isolation; (b) the extent to which the strategy can defuse some of the regional tensions; (c) the ability of the outcast to reduce economic and military dependence on the United States; (d) the character of the United States-outcast relationship and the influence the outcast has over its major ally; (e) the likelihood of mobilizing internal support for a particular strategy; and (f) the personal inclinations of the members of the outcasts' ruling elites.

The test of the national strategy of any state has been its degree of success in securing its own demands or resisting the demands of other powers. An outcast state must secure enough support to frustrate efforts to eliminate it as a political unit without closing the option for a regional detente.

### Entrenchment

This is a tempting option when no favorable changes can be foreseen in the hostile international environment (the arena of the exterior maneuver) or in the intensity of the politicide campaign. A small power can, indeed, ignore those international facts it cannot influence, and concentrate on a narrow range of vital interests (Keohane, 1971:163). While the outcast state cannot localize the conflict, it may choose to concentrate on countering the interior maneuver since the exterior maneuver usually culminates in an interior maneuver, i.e., military action. Each outcast state obviously must contemplate the possibility that it will be left alone to face a military threat at its borders.

To what extent is entrenchment, i.e., a policy of disregarding international and particularly United States' pressure to make any concessions viable? "Intransigence" may be complemented by higher risk policies to intimidate its rivals as well as its critical allies. A small power could affect its chances for survival by altering the expectations which other powers hold about its position and its likely response to external pressures (Rothstein, 1968:194).

The outcast states, not unexpectedly, regard international practices and resolutions as less binding and may be tempted to acquire "crazy state" dimensions (Dror, 1973). The outcast states are repeatedly denounced for breaking international norms. When an individual is publicly labeled as a rule breaker, he becomes highly suggestible (psychologically receptive) and may accept the proffered role of a particular kind of deviant as the only alternative (Scheff, 1966; Frazier, 1976:25-47). Possibly this acceptance of and conformity to negative expectations by the deviant person occurs also in groups, increasing the tendency for aggressive behavior by the outcast state. The reaction of Rhoodie Eschel, the South African Information Secretary, to an interviewer's question seems to confirm such a pattern of behavior. He said, "When you can't get a fair hearing in the world, morality flies out the window" (*Newsweek,* 2 April 1979:22).

On the other hand, status inconsistency would also result in aggressive policies. If the status attributed to a state by other national actors in the system is lower than self-perceived ranking, frustration is created in decision makers and the public. Such feelings toward aggressive international behavior persist as long as the discrepancy remains uncorrected (Wallace, 1973).

It is noteworthy that all four outcast countries are considered, as a group, to be potential transgressors against the international consensus against nuclear proliferation (Harkavy, 1981:135-63). A nuclear arsenal may appeal to an outcast state because such weapons could indicate to the world that the outcast is an international fact not easy to erase, and signal a resolve to charge a high price for any attempt to dissolve it. Some even claim that nuclear weapons could freeze the status quo and eliminate the danger of politicide. All four states have various potentials for military action to heighten regional tensions and to embarrass the United States (Evron, 1973:173-94; Baehr, 1975:459). Some Israelis, for example, savor the fact that they can, if it appears that

Israel may be sacrificed for oil, stop the oil flow (Sharon, 1975). Indeed, Israel under Prime Minister Begin and his defense minister, Sharon, adopted in the 1980s a more destabilizing strategic posture than before. It increased its inclination for preemptive strikes. To increase its deterrence, Israel had recourse to greater amounts of military force than before and used it more often (Inbar, 1983:32-49).

Adopting an entrenchment strategy may serve additional purposes. First, ignoring the international front may save the frustration of constantly battling the opponent's automatic majority in all international forums. Even considering the likely damage in relations with the United States, an entrenchment posture may be popular. The relationship of the outcast with the United States is ambivalent; dependence upon the United States is seen as necessary but American pressures are resented. Therefore a hard line approach may be welcome and may even boost national morale. The Likud election victory in May 1977 in Israel was partly due to resentment of the Carter administration's pressure on the Labor-led government. Vorster's hard line party in South Africa was victorious in the 1977 election for similar reasons. The hard line policy received a vote of confidence again in October 1978 when Botha was elected to succeed Vorster as Prime Minister of South Africa. Botha did not hesitate to embarrass the United States occasionally; for example, he deliberately dramatized the announcement of spying charges against the United States and the subsequent expulsion of three American military attachés in March 1979. Botha's disclosure could also have damaged the intelligence capacity of the United States in that area as well as its relations with some sub-Sahara African nations that were subject to the surveillance of the spying plane. On the other hand, Botha relaxed some race regulations and cooperated to some extent with the West when dealing with Rhodesia and even with Namibia.

Second, an entrenchment strategy may direct the national resources and ingenuity to counter the interior maneuver instead of wasting efforts in the international arena. For example, Prime Minister Vorster did not hesitate to close down the Department of Information, which was established to bolster the government's sagging image abroad, a decision that was due also to bureaucratic intrigues (The New York Times, 1978:6). In Israel, Begin and Dayan, his foreign affairs minister, decided not to react to every denunciation in an international forum. Israel's indignant responses, the government argued, could only please the Arabs (Maariv, 20 June 1979).

Third, such a strategy, if carried out for some time without too great a cost, may frustrate the outcast's enemies and may eventually bring them to accept the status quo or only slight changes in it.

Fourth, an argument can be made that United States' support will not, at least in the short run, dissipate in response to entrenchment; the pariah may have enough influence in the United States to prevent it. Under certain circumstances, a show of toughness can even improve the outcast's image in American public opinion. In addition, American strategic interests may force continued support. Drastic changes in American policy are in any case unlikely and it is more realistic to expect a gradual reduction in support. Indeed, only slight changes toward Israel can be detected in Washington in spite of the widespread criticism of and the occasional sanctions against Israeli policies under Begin. Time may be important; the longer a weak state has existed, the less the danger of its demise. Poland, once divided, made future partitions easier. Similarly, it was easy to liquidate the independence of small new states like the Baltic states because of their newness.

As a short-term policy, entrenchment is available to all outcast states. As a long-range policy, its success is greatly dependent upon the balance of resources between the besieged state and its enemies, as well as on the degree of utilization of those resources. Few nations are truly independent with no need for outside support or relations. The resources of the rivals of the outcast states are augmented, however, by extra-regional powers. Even the PRC is shopping for foreign investments and technology, as well as modern weapons, with some success. On the other hand, an entrenchment strategy is, of course, not conducive to generating support from the West under the present international circumstances.

In comparison to the pre-1973 period, the magnitude of the value of United States weaponry shipped to Israel has increased considerably. In 1972 Israel imported arms worth $453 million (constant to 1978), while in 1973 the figure was $329 million. In comparison, the figures for 1974, 1975, 1976, 1977 and 1978 were, respectively, $1,241 million; $864 million; $1,106 million; $1,177 million and $925 million (ACDA, 1982:No. 112). Since 1974, the yearly total of American military and economic aid to Israel has been around $2.2 billion (current dollars).

The amount of economic aid to Israel has also increased in part to alleviate the burden of the regional arms race. Israeli dependence upon American weapons, which are unavailable in local industries, however, cannot be eliminated. Moreover, even locally designed weapons systems need American capital and know-how to enable production (Inbar, 1982:45-48).

Yet this dependence is not continuous. Weapons are designed to last a few years; once new weapons systems are acquired, a country is less vulnerable to difficulties in future weapons procurement. A supplying country may hold its client on a short leash in terms of the number of units and spare parts, but this can be partially overcome by accumulation or indigenous production. The crucial points in time, in terms of dependence, are when equipment has to be replaced due to combat wear or because of modernization needs. Therefore a well-equipped Israel, which probably can prevent a military victory of any coalition of Arab countries, may have in the short run greater freedom of political action. It may choose what the United States and others possibly view as an intransigent policy. Indeed, the American suspension of aircraft deliveries in 1981 and 1982 seemed to have little effect on Israel, since the Israel Defense Forces could manage without those items for some time. In the long run, however, Israel's military superiority is not assured without United States support, especially in a period following another Middle East war. In a postwar period Israel will again need United States aid to pay for the war and to re-equip its military.

South Korea can ill afford to estrange the United States with an entrenchment strategy that may result in an immediate reduction of American military support, for the American military presence carries great political significance. South Korea will probably be reluctant to supply a pretext to those who favor American troop withdrawal, a move that would increase chances of an invasion by its northern opponent. North Korea seems to have a better army than its southern neighbor, but South Korea with its greater manpower resources and its industrial base can ultimately develop, with American aid, a satisfactory force to face the army of North Korea (Clough, 1976:6-17). American troops, however, will still be needed to deter Chinese or Soviet intervention.

Taiwan may choose entrenchment, since it may believe it has little to lose after the American severance of diplomatic ties and the abrogation of the United States-Taiwan treaty. Taiwan does not need any more American economic assistance. Moreover, this outcast state is rebuilding its military forces and being an island has a good chance to repel a PRC invasion without American troops (Cline, 1977:81; Cooper, 1977:268-69). Yet the modernization of its forces requires modern weapons not always available on the free market. For example, even the purchase of jets produced by another outcast—the Israeli Kfirs—are subject to an American veto. The Taiwanese are obviously interested, in the absence of another ally, in preserving the limited American commitment to sell them military equipment. Even congressional intention to maintain such a commitment as the Taiwan Relations Act demonstrated that it can be, and has been, frustrated by the

U.S. government's arms selling procedures. The Carter administration seemed unwilling to carry out the intention of the Taiwan Relations Act (Gregor, 1980:609-23; Gregor and Chang, 1980:3-25). In addition, a cardinal interest of the Taiwanese government is to keep Western markets open for its exports.

The entrenchment strategy seems to have a better chance for success in South Africa than in other outcast states. It is immensely richer than the others and is also outdistancing its African opponents in economic and military power. A military coalition of African countries, even with Cuban or East European support, faces considerable difficulties in an encounter with the well-equipped and well-trained South African army. Geography also does not favor the invader from the north because of the inhospitable deserts. Until African countries can develop a serious invading capacity, South Africa is free to develop its local arms industry. Weapons that cannot be acquired on the world market, because of an effective arms boycott, may be produced with some effort at home. The South African army has presently less to fear from a conventional military exchange than from guerrilla warfare inside South Africa. (In contrast, Israel, Taiwan and South Korea do not face any serious guerrilla activities.) An adequate military response to such a threat is much less dependent upon imported sophisticated jet aircraft or tanks that may be subject to an arms embargo.

The ruling Afrikaaner Nationalist party is probably psychologically more disposed to accept an entrenchment strategy than the ruling elites in the other outcast states. South Africa has traditionally pursued an isolationist foreign policy. The Afrikaaners may return (figuratively and actually) to a ''laager'' (stockade) mentality to defend their position (Carter, 1977:134). In addition, many seem to sincerely hold that if the Bantustan homelands policy is carried out as planned, the problem will be solved; the blacks will be citizens of other countries with no claims for civil rights in South Africa.

A possible corollary of an entrenchment strategy is the development of what Harold Laswell called a ''garrison state.'' Indeed, some observed increased militarization of South African society. Yet, the Israeli case indicates that a high perception threat and high levels of defense spending over years do not necessarily militarize a society (Horowitz, 1977:58-75).

In conclusion, the entrenchment strategy assumes that no changes in the outcast status are foreseeable, but it is viable only as a short-run strategy, since the isolated outcast states (with the exception, to some extent, of South Africa) lack the resources to sustain such a policy.

**Accommodation of the United States**

With the exception of South Africa, the outcast states seem less than certain that the immediate future is on their side. They prefer, therefore, to delay as long as possible the rift with the United States. The exterior maneuver seems more threatening for them than for South Africa. "Accommodation" is adopted by a state when its leadership perceives a grave threat to the state's interests and decides it must surrender (or forego something valuable) "in order to preserve other things of value, or in order to gain time, or in order to avoid additional defense expenditures or a risky war" (Karsten, 1976:158-59). In our case, the outcast states are demanded to go along with plans for a Pax Americana in order not to endanger United States support.

The outcast may demand as a quid pro quo for its docility a long-range commitment for economic and military support, and a formal incorporation into the Western alliance. The advantage of an accommodation strategy lies in the minimization of tensions with the United States. The image of the outcast as a docile ally may also strengthen its position in American public opinion and facilitate an even more comprehensive American commitment. Such a strategy may be adopted when the outcast has little or no influence over the United States and fears that the lack of cooperation may lead to its abandonment.

Another possible advantage is at the regional level. The concessions required by the United States might also reduce regional tensions. Moreover, accommodation of the United States could be accompanied by a more conciliatory policy toward the outcasts' regional opponents. For example, Israel, in addition to withdrawing from occupied territories, could abandon its retaliatory response to terrorist acts. Accommodation at the regional level could encourage moderation in the outcasts' rival countries.

The ruling elite may have difficulty in mobilizing popular support for what may be described as "appeasement" or "surrender" to United States pressures. Each country's tolerance level of interference plays an important part when considering this strategy (Cottam, 1967:34-77).

The crucial question for the outcast state's decision makers when analyzing the option of accommodation is what kinds of demands the Americans are presenting, and what kinds of solutions they are envisioning to the conflict the outcast is involved in. Moreover, it should be made clear what actions the Americans are willing to undertake to assure the success of the regional plans they have in mind.

In the Middle East, for example, Israel under Rabin (1974-1977) was more pro-American than any previous Israeli government. Nevertheless, the Israeli conception of a regional agreement was different from the American one (Steinberg, 1977:70-82). Even in return for Israeli withdrawal to 1967 lines, with minor rectifications, as the Americans want, the United States has not been willing to compensate the Israeli sense of insecurity by incorporating Israel into its alliance system. Even if it did, the credibility of such a commitment is shaky.

The United States wants to extricate itself from its alliances with South Korea and Taiwan. Presently, a complete troop withdrawal from South Korea would be interpreted by all in the area as a desertion of that ally. The South Koreans cannot be expected to go along with such a policy, especially since they perceive the North Korean army to be superior (Kang, 1977:167-81).

The United States' desire for "normalization" with the People's Republic of China met similar resistance, since the United States formally accepted Taiwan as legitimately representing the Chinese. A "German formula" could have been the only realistic solution to the Chinese impasse. Such a policy could have been tolerable even to Taiwan. But the one-China (Peking) American orientation was too difficult for the Taiwanese to accept.

The South Africans, too, cannot accept the American scenario of granting full equal rights to the nonwhite population. The American prescription, which is colored by their own problem with a black *minority* striving for equal civil rights, is rejected by most whites and even the "enlightened" ones.

None of the outcast states can fully go along with the American preferences. Even a generous supply of military hardware and massive economic aid cannot make the American scenario acceptable. Implementation of the American "solution" would lead to the liquidation of Taiwan and of the sovereignty of the "white tribe" in Southern Africa.

Israel and South Korea similarly perceive, not without justification, American plans as a threat to their mere existence. An accommodation strategy may bring American disengagement even closer. After granting the needed concessions—after being used—the isolated state would have even less value as an ally.

Accommodation, despite the promise for continuous Western support as well as some defusion of the regional conflict, is less attractive than entrenchment because the United States favors solutions unacceptable to the shunned nations.

### Realignment
United States policy seems to be drifting into greater conflict with the outcast states. In case the outcast state loses American support, can it

then find support in the Soviet Union? Is realignment a feasible strategy in order to counter the exterior maneuver? "Realignment" with the Soviet Union may open a new route of supply for sophisticated weapons and financial aid. Such a realignment may also enable the outcast to project a different image. The American imperialist image may give way to a progressive one. This may reverse the process of isolation. In addition, realignment may deny the enemy resources previously at its disposal.

The first difficulty in initiating such a drastic change in the outcast's foreign policy is an internal one. In spite of certain anti-American feelings, the citizens of the outcast states oppose a pro-Soviet orientation. Israel and white South Africa have democratic regimes and the voters are not likely to support a posture that can be easily viewed as "adventuristic" or "callous." Taiwan and South Korea, although not as democratic, permit considerable participation in the political process, and public opinion has to be taken into consideration.

The second difficulty, and the greater one, is the slim chance that the Soviet Union would cooperate in such a realigned posture. The outcast state has become isolated, precisely because of its problematic value as an ally. The Soviet Union has not hesitated to drop a client and pick up another one in cases in which it perceives a possible gain. In the Middle East, the Kurds, Communist parties and the Somalis found themselves deserted by the Soviet Union. Will the Soviet Union gain something by allying itself with one of the outcast states?

In the Middle East, a Moscow-Jerusalem axis is highly improbable even if the Israeli Left were somehow to gain power. Mutual interests may arise as the struggle of Ethiopia against its Arab neighbors and dissidents indicated. A Syrian turn to the West, in a Sadat manner (which means to Israel a threat of its continued occupation of the Golan Heights) may create another instance for tacit cooperation. Yet the Soviet Union does not need Israel to assure its presence in the Middle East. It can always find an important Arab country to side with in the inter-Arab conflicts. Moreover, due to Arab numbers, geography, and riches, they are more attractive allies to the Soviet Union than Israel is.

The Soviet Union has mutual interests with Taiwan in limiting the power of the PRC (Gurver, 1978:751-66). Taiwan may serve the Russians as a possible second front and as a bargaining chip with Peking (and even the United States). It may even be willing to cooperate militarily with Taipei, if that does not entail a high political price. But it is unlikely to undertake diplomatic relations, or officially recognize it.

It is plausible that if North Korea were to become closely identified with Peking, the Soviet Union would prefer to see a strong South Korea rather than a united pro-Chinese Korea. It is unlikely, however, that the Soviet Union would reciprocate a South Korean flirtation with massive aid, matching a similar Chinese program in the north.

South Africa is a greater political liability as an ally than any of the outcast states. It is very difficult to imagine a scenario in which the Soviet Union and South Africa could engage in conspicuous cooperation.

The outcast state cannot use effectively the threat to realign as leverage against the United States. Such a threat is not credible. As far as the outcast state is concerned, it exists largely in a unipolar system (Rothstein, 1968:22-28). It is within the United States' sphere of influence and it cannot ally itself with other powers.

Realignment would be acceptable only in the case of abandonment by the United States; only following such a desertion could the frustrated pro-Western public opinion support realignment. Even if adopted, realignment has little chance for success because of the questionable value of the outcast state. Taiwan is in the best position to receive some Soviet support, because it faces the PRC, a rival of the Soviet Union, and also because of its minimal needs.

## The Mixed Strategy

The outcast state cannot fully accommodate United States desires without seriously endangering its existence, but at the same time it needs American support to assure its existence, since, because of its minimal value on the international market, it cannot find another ally to support it. Yet the outcast does have some influence over the United States, and this may enable it to resist full accommodation or delay it. It can adopt a mixed strategy, which includes elements of the strategies discussed above. A mixed strategy is primarily an exterior maneuver to assure minimal support for the outcast state at the multilateral level. The focus of this strategy, however, is the bilateral relations with the United States. The primary goal is to keep alive the American commitment to provide vital supplies of weapons and/or funds, as well as to neutralize direct intervention of other great powers. A secondary goal is to reduce regional tensions.

Implementing such a strategy means minimizing the scope of the conflict of interests between the outcast and the United States. Operationally, a mixed strategy requires skillful use of the outcast's limited influence over the United States, as well as a thoughtful approach in making concessions to complement the basic resistance to American demands.

63

The first source of influence is the character of the American political process, which enables a well-organized lobby to have a considerable impact on the decision-making process (Truman, 1951; Cohen, 1973). The Israelis, for example, with the support of American Jewry, have organized a powerful lobby which exerts significant influence, though its extent has often been exaggerated. In the future, as in the past, the ability of the pro-Israel lobby to affect policy is likely to be limited to those issues—particularly military aid issues—on which the U.S. Congress has a determining voice (Trice, 1977:137). Yet, when ethnicity is a clear obstacle to United States foreign policy, its influence dissipates under the weight of national interest (Horowitz, 1977:177). Indeed, the Jewish lobby lost two significant battles in Congress. It failed in its opposition to the sale of F-15 fighter planes to Saudi Arabia in 1978 and in preventing the sale of AWACs (Airborne Warning and Control Systems), again to Saudi Arabia, in 1981. The Taiwanese, Korean and South African lobbies are also active in Washington. The South Koreans and the South Africans were so eager to secure a supportive climate that they engaged in legally dubious methods. The Koreans attempted to bribe American politicians (Koreagate) and South Africa was accused of attempting to illicitly influence the line of several American newspapers.

In addition, public opinion seems to be more influential in the United States than in other democracies because of the characteristics of the American political system and its institutional culture. Small allies can influence public opinion through propaganda. Israel appeals to many Americans because it is a democracy, an immigrant nation with a pioneering heritage facing overwhelming odds, and because of the Holocaust (Safran, 1978:571-76; Trice, 1977:443-63). Israel, though it is increasingly criticized, is more fortunate than the other outcast states in terms of its image in American public opinion. American politicians have often stated their commitment to a "special" relationship between Israel and the United States. The content of the "specialness" is not clear. Moreover, as in the case of Britain, the "special" relationship with Israel does not preclude tense relations and even occasionally a sense of betrayal (Neustadt, 1970; Kissinger, 1965). Yet a genuine sense of closeness and sympathy to the Jewish state can be discerned, although pro-Israel sentiment seems to be in decline.

Because of the responsiveness of the American political system to demands of interest groups and the widespread American sympathy for Israel, the initiation and implementation of decisions objectional to Israel, such as the refusal to supply weapons or the arming of Israel's foes, require great effort on the part of the U.S. administration. Indeed, it required heavy presidential lobbying to secure senate approval to sell Saudi Arabia F-15s in 1978 and AWACs in 1981. Since the American public opinion has become an important arena of the exterior maneuver of the opponents of the international outcasts, it has become a primary target for the outcast states' propaganda machines.

The United States' support for the outcasts stems also from strategic considerations. Benefits to the United States for supporting Israel indeed outweigh the stress this connection puts on United States-Arab relations. A good case has been made that the United States' friendship with Israel has marginal influence on the Arab stand toward the United States (Dowty, 1970:312-20). Conflict with Israel is only one of many factors that mold the Arab position toward America. Second, Israel helps the survival of pro-Western regimes in the Middle East, Jordan being the notable example. As well, Israel strengthens Western military capabilities in this important region; the country's military infrastructure, its air force, navy and ground forces, are an important contribution to the Western alliance. This has become particularly important after the 1974 Cyprus crisis, which caused a serious weakening of the southern NATO (North Atlantic Treaty Organization) flank. The Soviet invasion of Afghanistan and the instability in the Persian Gulf area, also indicate a growing need for Western bases in the territory of a stable ally east of the Mediterranean. And Israel's political stability is an asset for the Western alliance; it is a more reliable ally than any other Middle East nation. The political course of other regional actors is fraught with uncertainties. The emergence of a regime hostile to Western interests in countries like Saudi Arabia, Egypt, Turkey or Greece, is not a far-fetched scenario. The Iranian turn is a vivid example. The emergence of less cooperative governments in Italy and France, where the Left is very strong, is also possible. Finally, even if Israel's existence were indeed a burden for the United States, its demise might be infinitely worse (Dowty, 1970:320). To a great extent, United States' support to Israel and the other outcast states is a test of the United States' credibility as an ally and a world power.

Some Americans perceive the struggle of Israel in historiosophic terms. An attack on Israel is viewed as a confrontation between Western civilization, democracy and its humanistic values, and non-Western authoritarian philosophy. Support for Israel is therefore more than helping a strategically important, "nice" country—it is a moral imperative to save the embattled Western civilization (Fairlie, 1977:18-20, 22, 23; Wildavsky, 1977:5-13; Moynihan, 1978; Horowitz, 1976:361-91).

Among the outcast states, Israel seems to have the greatest leverage with the United States. In addition, like other outcasts, Israel can influence the United States into continuing economic aid and supply of weapons through two types of calculated concessions, and can gain time by shrewdly bargaining the scope and timing of concessions. The first type, concession to the outcasts' opponents, temporarily defuses to some extent the regional conflict. This also makes the support of the outcast less a political, military and economic burden. Among the outcast states, Israel has the greatest latitude in making concessions to its enemies. It can evacuate territories occupied in 1967. It can also make political concessions as to the Palestinian issue and the type of interim agreements reached in the absence of a formal peace treaty. South Africa can also make territorial concessions. It can give up Namibia or even parts of the territory of South Africa (this is actually its Bantustan policy). It can also allow greater freedom to its nonwhite population as a gesture to sub-Saraha Africa. South Africa also has the resources to offer economic aid to needy African countries in return for a less hostile posture. Selective regional concessions may in some instances split the opponents' coalition, *divide et impera*—alleviating to some extent the external threat. Israel's concessions to Egypt in 1975 and 1979 were directed to prevent the reemergence of the 1973 Egyptian-Syrian alliance. South Africa could court the moderate African countries to prevent effective cooperation with the radical states.

The second type of concession is on the bilateral level to the United States. The outcast may give in to certain American demands in order to reduce tensions or to foster some good will before presenting its "shopping list," or to get something in return. The United States, for example, is interested in nonproliferation of nuclear weapons. All four outcast states have been suspected of having intentions to acquire nuclear power capability. Consequently, they may want something in return for restraining their nuclear programs. Korea agreed to cancel the purchase of a plutonium separation plant from France in exchange for greater U.S. understanding of its security needs and domestic political problems. Israel, it was reported, acquiesced to United States "visits" to the Dimona reactor in exchange for modern weapons (Hodes, 1968:231-36; Beaton, 1969:11; Inbar, 1982:81-106). The Israeli lobby was asked, for example, to refrain from actively supporting the "Jackson amendment" concerning free immigration from the Soviet Union, or from opposing the Panama Canal treaties. In 1984 Israel was asked to station Voice of America equipment on its soil to facilitate broadcasts to the Soviet Union. Korea was asked to cooperate in the Koreagate scandal and in a scheduled limited United States troop withdrawal. All four outcasts could make gestures to placate occasional U.S. "human rights" concerns.

In spite of the fact that the outcast's survival serves to some extent as a test for United States' credibility as an ally, the ostracized state, in contrast to other weak allies, does not possess any "coercive deficiency," i.e., the outcast state cannot successfully threaten to collapse unless American support is increased (Halberstam, 1972:484-510; Rothstein, 1968, 119-20; Hoffman, 1968:4). The United States may refuse the increase as part of a disengagement policy or due to a dispute as to the real needs of the outcast. Similarly, a dramatic appeal for support may amplify the perception that the outcast is a burden for the United States. President Park of Korea recognized, for example, that it would be unwise to adopt a bargaining posture over U.S. withdrawals that overemphasized Korea's weakness relative to the North. This could have strengthened public sentiment in America in favor of withdrawals.

Outcast states may lack "coercive deficiency," but they do have another option. The outcast can credibly threaten to embarrass its ally—the United States—by taking some military action. The outcast can adopt some elements of an entrenchment strategy; it can heighten regional tensions and even provoke war. Israel, for example, can hint that unless the United States supplies a new generation of weapons it may have to start a preventive war in order to annihilate the potential threat of the developing Arab armies. The nuclear option can also be loudly considered, to American displeasure.

The mixed strategy contains elements of entrenchment, realignment and accommodation. Taiwan and South Korea may have the option to incorporate in such a strategy a limited dimension of realignment. Each country obviously needs a different mix to secure continuous United States support. Yet any outcast adopting this strategy has to control its built-in tensions. First, the outcast state's goals and those of its ally are incompatible (there may be, however, agreement on short-run objectives). Second, in order to make the United States pay a higher price for the concessions requested, the outcast may adopt a temporary entrenchment posture, which strains its relationship with the United States. Third, the concessions bartered for continuous American support may weaken its future bargaining position, although it may increase the freedom of action of the ostracized state in the short run. In addition, a mixed strategy may face another problem: it is difficult to build a wide national consensus for a policy fraught with contradictions. The government can always be accused of weakness or inconsistency. Democracies such as Israel and South Africa face greater constraints of domestic politics.

67

The mixed strategy, despite its internal contradictions, seems to be the most promising option for the international outcast. It may secure continuous support, without too great a security risk. It also minimizes regional tensions and in the case of Israel, South Korea and even South Africa, it allows conditions for possible exit from outcast status.

**Table 2**
**Strategies for Outcast States**

| Strategies | Assumptions About International Environment | Strategy Goals | | Policy Content | Resources Needed | Who Can Apply Strategy |
|---|---|---|---|---|---|---|
| | | Primary | Secondary | | | |
| Entrenchment | Attitudes at regional & global level; hostile, but little impact on national security | Preservation status quo | Continuous Western support | No concessions to regional adversaries or west; disregard of international resolutions, and western public opinion; inclination to high-risk policies; retaliatory policy; publicity to nuclear option; emphasis on regional nuisance potential | Independent military & economic capabilities superior to regional coalitions | South Africa; others just short-run |
| Accommodation | Attitudes at regional & global level; hostile, dangerous to national security/slight changes in both possible, particularly in Western attitudes | Continuous Western support | Reduction in politicide intensity (regional detente) | Acceptance of Pax Americana; concessions to the U.S. and regional exchange for American guarantees of long range economic military and political substantial support; emphasis on public relations attempting to project an image of a faithful ally | Pax Americana not inimical to mere survival; something the U.S. wants | Israel, South Korea |
| Realignment | Attitudes at regional & global level; hostile, dangerous to national security; change possible at global level; as result slight changes possible in regional attitudes | Preservation of status quo | Exit from outcast status | Looking for a new source of support by courting the Soviet Union; disregard of Western public opinion | A common enemy with the Soviet Union and/or something the Soviet Union wants | Taiwan, South Korea (?) |
| Mixed Strategy | Attitudes at regional & global level; hostile, dangerous to national security; slight changes in both possible | Continuous Western support | Regional detente | Tacit rejection of Pax Americana, protracted bargaining of limited and gradual concessions in return for American economic military and political support; sensitivity to Western public opinion coupled with willingness to absorb occasional setbacks as result of its refusal to accommodate the U.S.; subtle threats to adopt entrenchment or realignment | Divisible goods the U.S. wants | Israel, South Africa, Taiwan, South Korea |

# 4

## CONCLUSION

This work has examined an unusual phenomenon in the international politics of the post-World War II period—the outcast state. These states—Israel, South Africa, Taiwan and South Korea—face opponents who try to eradicate them as political entities by refusing to grant legitimacy to them and by conducting diplomatic, economic and military campaigns against them.

Yet, regional politicide, a characteristic of the regional conflict in which they are involved, is not enough to successfully isolate a state; worldwide cooperation is needed. In the 1960s and 1970s, the outcasts' rivals emerged from global changes with greater political leverage than before, which enabled them to mobilize enough multilateral support to accelerate the process. The loosening of bipolarity, the emergence of a more coordinated Third World and the decline of the United States as a global power combined to weaken the outcast states. Their opponents were backed by communists or belonged to the stronger Third World coalition.

In addition to the politicide campaign and the uneasy international constellation, Western support declined. The strategic contribution of outcast states to the West was questioned, and the strategic importance ascribed to them fluctuated according to changing international circumstances. A Vietnam-weary America in retreat, displaying isolationist tendencies, placed less value on marginal embattled allies.

Further, the outcast states displayed an ethno-cultural marginality which further reduced the chances of continued American support. None of these states could be comfortably classified from an ethno-cultural point of view as white European (not even the "white tribe" in South Africa). On the other hand, the economically developed outcast states were handicapped because non-Western nations perceived them as Western outposts.

A convergence of several factors—the regional politicide against the outcast, its national characteristics, and the changes in the international system—contributed to the emergence of the outcast state. As a result, outcast states are not treated as legitimate members of the international community. Most states are reluctant to maintain conspicuous diplomatic, economic or cultural relations with the outcasts and increasingly exclude them from multilateral interactions in the international system.

The outcast state, a new international actor, can be viewed as a subcategory of the small state. The outcast states belong to the small state category by their dimensions (South Africa is to some extent an exception, but only in terms of territory) and capabilities. Moreover, their system-determining capability is very limited, a characteristic of small states (Keohane, 1969:295-96). The outcast states have very little ability to initiate or affect systemic changes. Further, like other small states, the outcast cannot solve its security problems without outside support.

Yet the outcast is distinct from other small states in the contemporary international system by the peculiarity of the problem it faces. Rothstein claims that the small state "is not defined by specific qualities, which it possesses (or lacks), but by a position it occupies in its own and other eyes" (Rothstein, 1968:7). This is also true of the outcasts. Obviously, the marginality of the outcast is not unparalleled, in spite of the fact that it is a contributing factor to outcast status. Yet its isolation is unique. In addition, the character of its regional conflict, politicide, is uncommon. Moreover, the threat to the outcast's existence (with the possible exception of Taiwan) does not come from first-or second-rate powers but from regional, less powerful, enemies.

The outcast state, being a Western ally, differs from the small state also because the systemic changes of the 1960s affected it differently than other small states, particularly those belonging to the Third World. The loosening of bipolarity at the regional level and the greater international leverage of Third World actors increased small powers' freedom of action. Regional objectives, once considered unachievable because they are linked to the superpowers' confrontation, were now within the reach of the smaller states without any of the previous global implications and the danger of escalation. Moreover, small powers in a regional subsystem can mobilize superpower support, particularly Soviet support, in the light of the American redefinition of its global interests, without arousing similar support of the other superpower for its adversaries. Cuba's actions in Central America and Africa, and Vietnam's deeds in Laos and Cambodia follow such a pattern. In the changed international system the outcasts' opponents could appeal to several sources of support, even to America, to augment their capability, without triggering corresponding support for the outcast. Moreover, the resort to force encounters less political difficulties for Third World countries than for Western powers.

The diminished competition between the superpowers was beneficial for most small states (Oren, 1980:111-19). It increased the range of available policies, without drastically reducing their bargaining power to secure superpower support for their policies.

In contrast to the effect on other small powers, the emergence of a more diffuse system actually worsened the outcast's situation. Theoretically, the outcast, too, had now to worry less about the global implications of its actions. Yet, being status quo powers, the outcasts were not so much concerned with their own freedom of action as with the actions of their opponents. In spite of the revisionist image their opponents propagate, the pariahs have limited ambitions and basically strive only to defend their own territory. Israel is very reluctant to withdraw from some parts of the territories conquered in 1967 but has no plans whatsoever to expand. South Africa has no desire to acquire additional territories. South Korea, explicitly, and Taiwan, implicitly, abandoned the goal of national unification and are willing to settle for a partition formula. The outcasts' rivals are actually the revisionist powers; a less structured system and its greater leeway for small states favors these powers.

Moreover, Israel, Taiwan, South Korea and even South Africa worry more about their *capability* for action than about their *range* of action, particularly their defensive capability, i.e., the ability to hold their territories. Enhancing this capability could free the outcast from international pressures to make concessions to its rivals and raise the price of military intervention against it. The outcast's main objective, then, is to secure the support needed to obtain an adequate *capability* to withstand a regional onslaught. But its unattractiveness on the international market hinders this effort. Its rivals, by indirect strategy, have attempted to sever the outcast's links to the West, which could help acquire this support.

As long as the outcast's regional conflict had a bipolar dimension, it could secure some support from the United States. Reduced bipolarity weakened the bargaining power of all small states while it increased the superpowers' freedom of action. But the outcast's bargaining power was particularly damaged.

The outcast does not have much latitude in choosing its ally. With the possible exception of Taiwan, the outcasts act essentially as if they operate in a unipolar system. In the case of Israel, Taiwan and South

Korea, even renunciation of some degree of sovereignty and acceptance of satellite status is not attractive enough to the United States to secure the outcasts' existence. A strategy of accommodation is not effective in achieving the goal of national preservation.

Another difference between the small state and the outcast state lies in its relations with the IGOs. In international organizations, many matters are decided by a majority vote. As each state has one vote, the power differential between states is less marked. Such organizations have served to some extent to shield the small states (Keohane, 1969:298), which attempted to manipulate the organizations in their interests. Yet, international forums do not serve the same function for the outcast states. In fact, the IGOs are among the most dedicated international actors supporting the politicide campaign.

As argued, outcast states can do little to change their status. Only systemic changes and/or an end to politicide could "normalize" their situation. Yet, both factors are beyond the outcast's control. A stronger and more assertive West could eliminate doubts about its commitment to its allies. Greater fears of communist expansionism could similarly strengthen those outcasts interested in checking Soviet and/or Chinese advances. For example, greater attention to the bipolar dimension of world politics in the Arab world could modify Israel's opponents' foreign policy agenda and relegate the regional conflict with Israel to a lower priority, even though Israel or the other outcasts are powerless to bring about such changes.

Such a bipolar perception was probably one of the reasons for Sadat's initiative for a peace treaty with Israel. Sadat's trip to Jerusalem, possibly the beginning of the end of politicide for Israel, was indeed quite unexpected; it was neither the product of an Egyptian reconciliation process nor a function of Israeli foreign policy. Yet systemic factors precluded similar agreements with other Arab countries; the Egyptian policy was not adopted by the rest of Israel's Arab foes because of Egypt's diminished international role, as well as because of different threat perceptions. Similarly, a detente with Pretoria in Africa can be successfully initiated only by one of the more influential African international actors. Mozambique's 1984 pact with South Africa was not emulated by other African countries because Mozambique is not an important African actor.

Only the outcasts' opponents can relinquish politicide, as an internal decision, and the outcast can make only a limited contribution to such a psycho-historic process. The outcast needs some degree of sensitivity to its opponents, but what is needed above all is an unyielding determination not to surrender to a politicide campaign. But until China, North Korea and the important Arab and African states abandon politicide, the outcasts can only hope that systemic changes will alleviate their situation.

What can the outcast states do in the meantime? A strategy of accommodation is dangerous to their mere existence. A strategy of realignment, i.e., looking for another ally, is a remote possibility, which only Taiwan can contemplate. Entrenchment, which emphasizes noncooperation with other international actors and the outcast's nuisance value, is within reach of all as a short-range policy. All outcast states have the ability to heighten regional tensions to the point of war. South Africa could interdict oil shipments to the West, while Taiwan could do the same to Japan. Israel, above all, could destroy oil fields in the Middle East. But in the long run, entrenchment alienates the outcast's reluctant ally and risks losing its vital support. The mixed strategy is the most promising; it attempts to utilize the outcast's limited leverage to continue the vital relationship with the West.

Israel is perhaps in the worst position among the outcasts. The politicide campaign against it is the most comprehensive. It is the only outcast whose people, regime and state have been denied legitimacy. Moreover, the military threat to its existence is more real than that to the other outcasts. South Korea hosts American troops on its soil. The Formosa Strait is a formidable barrier to invasion of Taiwan. No African offensive against South Africa is in sight. In contrast, the Arab countries have, since the 1973 war, expanded their arms capability with the possibility of a new round of hostilities. The 1969 Egyptian-Israeli peace treaty has, in the short run, alleviated Israel's military and political situation, but has not drastically changed its strategic dilemma. The treaty is presently under strain and its future is uncertain. The treaty also challenges Israeli control of the West Bank, which is viewed as the most difficult area to relinquish because of its proximity to Israel's population centers. Moreover, the main threat to Israel in recent years has not been Egypt, but the potential Arab alliance on its eastern front.

What can we learn from the recent history of Israel and the other outcasts? Obviously, each outcast has its particular security problems, different political elites, predispositions and decision-making processes. Nevertheless, we can discern a pattern among them. None of the outcast states adopted an entrenchment strategy, even as a short-run option. It would appear that countries are not easily pushed into a "crazy state" posture by external pressures; all four maintained some measure of political cooperation with the United States. South Africa under Botha was expected to choose an entrenchment strategy, but preferred to be flexible on Rhodesia, Namibia, and even in its racial policies. The feelings of rage against the United States in deserted Taiwan could have generated an entrenchment strategy or a move toward realignment. However, Taiwan did not burn its bridges with the United States. Even Israel under Begin attempted to maintain a good relationship with America. Israel's acceptance of the American negotiated agreement for the withdrawal of foreign troops from Lebanon (May 1983) is an example of Begin's reluctance to exacerbate tensions with Washington.

Fears that an outcast state would achieve nuclear power status were premature and exaggerated. Neither Israel nor any of the other outcasts has gone nuclear. Even the derecognition of Taiwan by the United States, a quite dramatic international action, did not precipitate a Taiwanese quest for a nuclear force. Israel under the Begin administration adopted a greater degree of entrenchment in its foreign policy, but exerted the same caution on the nuclear issue as the previous Rabin government (Inbar, 1985). This is quite remarkable in light of nuclear developments in Iraq and Pakistan. Leaders of isolated states have long been preoccupied with security issues; they have been in contact with Western strategic thinking long enough to be sensitized to Western apprehensions of the political and military usefulness of nuclear weapons.

Israel under the Rabin and Begin administrations never considered becoming a formal nuclear power, but was very anxious to augment its conventional arsenal. All outcasts needed an improved conventional capability because of their rivals' more elaborate armament programs. The Arabs, some African states, the PRC and North Korea made great efforts to increase their military capabilities, posing a greater threat to the outcasts.

In order to build and maintain a military force large enough and sufficiently advanced to deter this threat, the outcast state needs modern weapons. The purchase of sophisticated weapons systems, particularly if they are expensive or highly visible (tanks and airplanes), is subject to the producer's government control and therefore becomes a political matter. The outcast's efforts to acquire the latest weapons in the West were therefore not only directed toward bettering its armed forces, but also to exploit the political overtones of weapons sales. For example, in the Middle East, Arabs considered the American-made Phantom jet a symbol of American commitment to Israel. The political value of arms deliveries also adds to the outcast's deterrent power, which has been weakened as support from the West in an emergency has become less probable. An assurance of such support could enhance the deterrence of Israel, Taiwan, Korea and even South Africa. A mixed force of African and Cuban (East German?) troops is more likely to operate against South Africa in a loosened subsystem than in a bipolar one.

All small states have small margins of security, but the outcast states, because of their opponents' radical goals, have even smaller ones. Therefore, in addition to upgrading their military defensive capabilities the outcast states must erect political obstacles to aggression, e.g., internationally sponsored agreements and an international force to supervise their implementation. Such agreements lend legitimacy to the status quo and make the politicide campaign politically more costly.

The outcast state, in addition to improving its deterrence by political and military means, has to try to achieve what Rabin called "strategic coordination" with the United States. For example, a more alert Taiwan, one astute enough to bargain openly for a "two-Chinas" policy in the early 1970s could possibly have achieved the necessary political understanding with the United States to prevent derecognition. Adhering on the declaratory level to the intention of recapturing the mainland, even though it appears that there was a realistic tendency in the high policy elite to accept a two-Chinas policy, was in retrospect an unsuccessful application of entrenchment, which played into the hands of the Communists in Peking. Similarly, the nationalistic bravado of Begin's settlement policy undermined the more convincing security arguments for Israeli control of the West Bank. His policy provoked United States' advice against settlement there in general. The outcast has no power to change the international constellation. Yet its policies can ameliorate or worsen its situation, particularly in the West.

A small state, if not in conflict with a superpower, usually maintains a regional perspective. The outcast, in spite of the fact that its rivals are regional powers, must have a global perspective (unless an entrenchment strategy is chosen). This is necessary to combat the opponents' objective, which is to internationalize the conflict. In particular, the outcast must counter perceptions that it is an unnecessary burden on the West, and that it has no right to exist.

Israel, and evidently the other outcasts as well, has neglected the normative aspect of the indirect strategy's ultimate goal—politicide. This was due to a predisposition to think primarily in terms of *realpolitik*. In addition, the intensity of their efforts to secure material and political aid from the West left the outcasts exhausted, with little energy remaining to deal with the avalanche of condemning epithets. Further, a small state's foreign policy machinery is limited and cannot handle too many fronts. Fighting the Soviet propaganda machine in particular and what Moynihan calls semantic infiltration is beyond the means of the small power. Nevertheless, greater attention to preventing erosion of legitimacy, at least in the West, could have been expected of the outcasts.

To what extent did isolation lead to closer relations among like outcast states? Harkavy (1977:644-48) has pointed out several limits to an outcast international. In spite of the fact that trade has increased dramatically among the outcast states, interpariah economic transactions could hardly substitute for a trading relationship with the West.

Could interpariah cooperation be more significant in the area of national security? There has been considerable speculation about a nuclear link between Israel and South Africa, or even between Taiwan and South Korea, but in the absence of any hard evidence, such cooperation remains a matter of pure conjecture. Moreover, as pointed out earlier, the nuclear option is not necessarily the preferred solution to the outcasts' security problems.

Conventional weapons procurement is the critical area of concern in these countries. Complementary efforts on the part of the outcast states, however, cannot easily overcome the technological and economic problems connected with the design and production of highly advanced aircraft and tanks. Israeli sales of military hardware to South Africa (missile patrol boats and other military items) and to Taiwan (Shafrir air-to-air missiles and Gabriel sea-to-sea missiles) obviously benefited all concerned and particularly the Israeli military industries. Yet Israel's production of the Kfir and Lavi airplanes and the Merkava tank has been contingent upon an American transfer of technology and even funds. Most significantly, the engines for these planes and tanks are American, and American acquiescence is needed for the sale of any equipment that includes American components. The United States has been reluctant to allow the development of military industries that would reduce the leverage upon recipients of American arms, or would compete with its own hard-pressed military industries. The Israeli-made Kfir with its American J-79 engine is a good illustration of American reluctance; permission to retransfer the J-79 has been rarely granted. Interestingly, American "public" approval of the sale of Kfirs to Taiwan (June 1978) put an end to any interest Taiwan might have had in such a transaction. The publicity surrounding sales of highly visible equipment such as airplanes was a burden even for another outcast state.

A closer look at Israeli conduct in the post-1973 period indicates a reluctance to form an alliance of the shunned. Israel never had diplomatic relations with Taiwan, whose claim to represent a territory it did not control was similar to the PLO position and did not appeal to Israel. Israel actually hoped that the Sino-American rapproachement would bring China closer to Israel—the anti-Soviet bastion in the Middle East. Like other countries, Israel preferred relations with the PRC to relations with Taiwan. Attempts to establish diplomatic relations with Peking were, however, not fruitful. Meanwhile, Taiwan did not want to trade its diplomatic ties with Saudi Arabia and Jordan, as well as its lucrative economic relations with the Arab world, for open cooperation with Israel.

In South Korea there has been sympathy for Israel; yet since 1970 no Korean diplomatic representative was assigned to Israel, in spite of the presence of an Israeli embassy in Seoul. Following the Yom Kippur War, the relations between Israel and South Korea became even cooler. In December 1973 the South Korean government made a pro-Arab declaration censoring Israeli retention of Arab territory and urging Israel to solve the Palestinian problem. Since then, whenever discussing the Middle East, they refer to this declaration. Like Taiwan, Korea is oil dependent and maintains a strong economic relationship with the Arab world. Israel has placed little importance on relations with Korea and in 1978 it closed its embassy in Seoul.

The only outcast with whom relations with Israel improved after 1973 was South Africa. Israel has had a consulate in Johannesburg since 1949, while South Africa opened its diplomatic legation in Tel-Aviv only in 1972. Israel had a constant interest in maintaining good relations with South Africa because of the large Jewish community there—the Jewish prism of Israel's foreign policy. Israel was bitterly disappointed by the severance of diplomatic relations by the sub-Sahara African nations after the October 1973 war. These two factors facilitated relations with South Africa. The two countries have complementary economies: Israel was interested in South African raw materials and markets and South Africa was a good potential customer of and investor in the Israeli arms industry. Indeed, a significant part of the increase in Israel's trade volume to South Africa was due to sales of military equipment. The growing economic cooperation expressed itself politically. In 1974, Israel raised the rank of its diplomatic mission in South Africa to embassy status. In 1976, the Israelis and Prime Minister Vorster agreed to greater South African-Israeli economic and scientific cooperation. The Israeli security establishment also displayed enthusiasm in developing relations with Pretoria (Hauser, 1979:75-82).

On the one hand, the strategic aspect of this relationship, i.e., Western outposts closing ranks to oppose Soviet schemes for the Indian Ocean and its shores, appealed to Israel's "power politics" way of thinking. On the other hand, Israel exerted greater caution in its contacts with South Africa in order to make itself less vulnerable to international criticism (particularly among friends). Following the Vorster visit, which attracted international attention, Israel adopted a lower profile. In light of Israel's low proportion of trade with South Africa (less than one percent of South Africa's total trade volume) and the small proportion of Israeli arms in the South African arsenal, talk of a Jerusalem-Pretoria axis is no more than a propaganda device of the indirect strategy employed by Israel's foes.

Israel never attempted to create an alliance among the outcasts as a lever against or as a substitute for the United States. The system-pervading inhibitions on cordial relations with an outcast state existed also in Israel. Similarly, Seoul and Taipei preferred not to be associated with Jerusalem. South Africa has displayed a willingness to approach other outcasts, possibly because it has been isolated longer than the others. It publicly courts Israel and Taiwan. (In contrast to Israel, Taiwan is more willing to formalize relations with South Africa, particularly after derecognition by the United States in 1978.)

It seems that as politico-military relations with the West deteriorate, one can discern a greater willingness to become an open partner in an international outcast association. Lesser inhibitions as a result of increased isolation, as well as a need to compensate for reduced or endangered American support, could bring a closer outcast states association (see Foisie, 1980).

The significance of an outcast state concept rests first at the descriptive level, as it gives a name to and defines the particular situation of several international actors. This work delineates the boundaries of this category. The outcast state is an isolated state in the international community subject to a politicide campaign. Since isolation is imposed in the case of the outcast, this concept allows us also to distinguish between various types of isolation.

The outcast concept is useful at the explanatory level as well. It explains how certain countries are treated in the international system after falling into an outcast condition. Since the analysis in this monograph is to a great extent systemic, the concept emphasizes the systemic factors that allowed the emergence of outcast status. Explaining the process of becoming an outcast and its predicament adds to our understanding of related issues in a loosened bipolar system, such as coalition formation dynamics, global interdependence, small states' capabilities and freedom of action, and alliance management.

This study has not dealt intensively with the actual policies of the outcast states. It seems, however, that there are great similarities in the outcasts' behavior, which can be explained by their belonging to this special group of states. Similarities in the areas of nuclear proliferation, alliance with the United States and weapons procurement programs have been noted. The national security policies of the outcasts deserve, however, a separate treatment, which is beyond the scope of this monograph. A comparative study of such policies could be an additional contribution to the outcast state concept.

Like most concepts and models in social science, the outcast concept has limited predictive value, although some projections for the ripe conditions to exit from the outcast state category can be made. Escape from outcast status is not conceivable unless systemic conditions change. The direction of such required change in the modern world means a more assertive United States and a more feared Soviet Union. In the absence of these international systemic changes, only the renunciation of the politicide campaign, a decision that can be made only by the outcasts' opponents, could bring about a change in outcast status. The continuation of the outcast status of the four countries will probably result in greater cooperation among them. As outcast status persists, inhibitions on forging relations with other outcasts decline and the emergence of a future outcast international becomes a possibility.

# REFERENCES

ACDA. 1982. *World Military Expenditures and Arms Transfers, 1970-1979.* United States Arms Control and Disarmament Agency, Pub. 112. Washington, D.C.: U.S. Government Printing Office.

Ajami, Fouad. 1980. The Fate of Nonalignment. *Foreign Affairs* 60:366-85.

Al Mashat, Abdul Monem. 1983. Egyptian Attitudes Toward the Peace Process; Views on an "Alert Elite." *Middle East Journal* 37:394-411.

Antonovsky, Aaron. 1956. Toward Refinement of the "Marginal Man" Concept. *Social Forces* 25:57-62.

Apter, David E., Ed. 1964. *Ideology and Discontent.* New York: Free Press.

Aron, Raymond. 1966. *Peace and War, A Theory of International Relations.* New York: Doubleday.

Baehr, Peter R. 1975. Small States: A Total for Analysis. *World Politics* 27:456-66.

Barnett, A. Doak. 1974. *Uncertain Passage.* Washington, D.C.: Brookings Institution.

Baromi, Joel. 1976. Latin American States' Conduct at the UN Assembly on Issues Affecting Israel. In *Israel and the Third World,* M. Curtis and S. Gitelson, eds., pp. 270-86. New Brunswick: Transaction Books.

Barrat, John. 1976. Southern Africa: A South African View. *Foreign Affairs* 55:147-68.

Bauer, P. T. 1976a. Western Guilt and Third World Poverty. *Commentary* 61:31-38.

_____. 1976b. Rev. ed. *Dissent on Development.* Cambridge: Harvard University Press.

Beaton, Leonard. 1969. Why Israel Doesn't Need the Bomb. *The New Middle East* 7:11-14.

Beaufre, Andre. 1970. *An Introduction to Strategy.* New York: Praeger.

Becker, Howard S. 1963. *The Outsiders.* New York: Free Press.

Bedeski, Robert E. 1983. *The Fragile Entente.* Boulder: Westview.

Berger, Peter L. 1976. The Greening of American Foreign Policy. *Commentary* 61:23-27.

Bergsten, C. Fred. 1973. The Threat from the Third World. *Foreign Policy* 11:102-24.

Binder, Leonard. 1958. The Middle East as a Subordinate International System. *World Politics* 10:408-29.

Bjöl, Erling. 1971. The Small State in International Politics. In *Small States in International Relations,* A. Schou and A. Brundtland, eds. Stockholm: Almqvist & Wiksell.

Boutros-Ghali, Boutros. 1982. The Foreign Policy of Egypt in the Post-Sadat Era. *Foreign Affairs* 61:769-813.

Brecher, Michael. 1972. *The Foreign Policy System of Israel.* London: Oxford University Press.

_____. 1974. *Decisions in Israel's Foreign Policy.* London: Oxford University Press.

Bryson, T. A. 1977. *American Diplomatic Relations with the Middle East, 1874-1975: A Survey.* Metuchen, New Jersey: Scarecrow Press.

Buchanan, W. and H. Cantrill. 1953. *How Nations See Each Other.* Urbana: University of Illinois Press.

Carr, Edward H. 1939. Propaganda in International Relations. *Oxford Pamphlets on World Affairs* 16:26.

Carter, Gwendolen M. 1977. South Africa: Battleground of Rival Nationalism. In *Southern Africa in Crisis,* G. M. Carter and Patrick O'Meara, eds. pp. 89-135. Bloomington: Indiana University Press.

Carter, Gwendolen M. and Patrick O'Meara, eds. 1977. *Southern Africa in Crisis: Bloomington: Indiana University Press.*

Cline, Ray S. 1977. *World Power Assessment 1977.* Boulder: Westview Press.

Clough, Ralph N. 1976. *Deterrence and Defense in Korea.* Washington, D.C.: Brookings Institution.

Cohen, Bernard C. 1973. *The Public's Impact on Foreign Policy.* Boston: Little, Brown.

Connell, George M. 1980. The Soviet Navy in Theory and Practice. *Comparative Strategy* 2:129-48.

Cottam, Richard W. 1967. *Competitive Interference and Twentieth Century Diplomacy.* Pittsburgh: University of Pittsburgh Press.

Curtis, Michael and Susan A. Gitelson, eds. 1976. *Israel and the Third World.* New Brunswick: Transaction Books.

Dagan, Avigdor. 1970. *Moscow and Jerusalem.* London: Abelard-Schuman.

Deibel, Terry L. 1978. A Guide to International Divorce. *Foreign Policy* 30:17-35.

Dowty, Alan. 1970. Does the United States Have a Real Interest in Supporting Israel? In *Great Issues of International Politics,* Morton A. Kaplan, ed., pp. 312-20.

Draper, Theodore. 1981. The Western Misalliance. *Washington Quarterly* 4:13-69.

Dror, Yehezkel. 1973. *Crazy States: A Counterconventional Problem.* Lexington: D.C. Heath.

Eschel, R. 1979. *Newsweek,* April 2:22.

Evron, Yair. 1973. *The Middle East.* New York: Praeger.

Fairbanks, Charles. 1976. War Limiting. In *Historical Dimensions of National Security Problems,* K. E. Knorr, ed. pp. 164-226. Lawrence: University of Kansas Press.

Fairlie, Henry. 1977. Epistle of a Gentile to Saul Bellow. *New Republic* 5:18-20, 22, 23.

Foisie, Jack. 1980. Israel, Taiwan and South Africa Form "Alliance of Shunned." *Los Angeles Times,* October 19.

Fomerand, Jacques. 1976. Changing Third World Perspectives and Policies Toward Israel. In *Israel and the Third World,* M. Curtis and S. Gitelson, eds., pp. 325-60. New Brunswick: Transaction Books.

Fox, Annette Baker. 1957. *The Power of Small States.* Chicago: University of Chicago Press.

Frazier, Charles E. 1976. *Theoretical Approaches to Deviance.* Columbus, OH: Charles E. Merrill.

Freedman, Robert O. 1975. *Soviet Policy Toward the Middle East Since 1970.* New York: Praeger.

Friedman, Milton. 1953. The Methodology of Positive Economics. In *Essays in Positive Economics,* M. Friedman, ed., pp. 3-43. Chicago: University of Chicago Press.

_____. 1980. Economic Sanctions. *Newsweek:* January 21:48.

Gati, Toby L. 1980. The Soviet Union and the North-South Dialog. *Orbis* 24:241-70.

Geertz, Clifford. 1964. Ideology as a Cultural System. In *Ideology and Discontent,* David E. Apter, ed., pp. 47-76. New York: Free Press.

Giboa, Moshe. 1969. *Six Years-Six Days.* Tel Aviv: Am Oved.

Gitelson, Susan A. 1976. Israel's African Setback in Perspective. In *Israel and the Third World,* M. Curtis and S. Gitelson, eds., pp. 182-99. New Brunswick: Transaction Books.

Goldberg, Milton M. 1940. A Qualification of the Marginal Man Theory. *American Sociological Review* 6:52-58.

Gregor, A. James. 1980. The United States, the Republic of China and the Taiwan Relations Act. *Orbis* 24:609-23.

Gregor, A. James and M. Hsia Chang. 1980. Arms Control, Regional Stability and the Taiwan Relations Act. *Journal of Strategic Studies* 3:3-25.

Gurver, John W. 1978. Taiwan's Russian Option: Image or Reality. *Asian Survey* 18:751-66.

Han, Sunjoo. 1978. South Korea 1977: Preparing for Self-Reliance. *Asian Survey* 18:45-50.

Harkabi, Yehoshafat. 1969. Fedayeen Action and Arab Strategy. *Alelphi Papers* 53:1. London: IISS.

_____. 1972. *Arab Attitudes to Israel.* Jerusalem: Israel University Press.

_____. 1977. *Arab Strategies and Israel's Response.* New York: Free Press.

Harkavy, Robert E. 1977. The Pariah State Syndrome. *Orbis* 21:623-49.

_____. 1981. Pariah States and Nuclear Proliferation. *International Organization* 35:138-42.

Harries, Owen. 1975. Australia's Foreign Policy Under Whitlam. *Orbis:* 102-24.

Hauser, Rita E. 1979. Israel, South Africa and the West. *Washington Quarterly* 2:75-82.

Hazan, Baruch A. 1976. *Soviet Propaganda. A Case Study of the Middle East Conflict.* Jerusalem: Keter.

Heikal, M. H. 1976. The Strategy of the War of Attrition. In *The Israel-Arab Reader,* 3rd. rev. ed., W. Laqueur, ed. pp. 414-26. New York: Bantam.

Hirschman, Albert O. 1970. *Exit, Voice and Loyalty.* Cambridge: Harvard University Press.

Hodes, Aubrey. 1968. *Dialogue with Ishmael.* New York: Funk & Wagnalls.

Hoffman, Stanley. 1968. *Gulliver's Troubles, or the Setting of American Foreign Policy.* New York: McGraw-Hill.

_____. 1970. International Organization and the International System. *International Organization* 24:401.

Holsti, K. J. 1974, 2nd. ed. *International Politics.* London: Prentice Hall.

Horowitz, Dan. 1977. Is Israel a Garrison State? *Jerusalem Quarterly* 4:58-75.

Horowitz, Irving L. 1966. *Three Worlds of Development: The Theory and Practice of International Stratification.* London: Oxford University Press.

_____. 1976. From Pariah People to Pariah Nation: Jews, Israelis, and the Third World. In *Israel and the Third World,* M. Curtis and S. Gitelson, eds., pp. 361-91. New Brunswick: Transaction Books.

_____. 1977. Ethnic Politics and United States Foreign Policy. In *Ethnicity and United States Foreign Policy,* A.A. Said, ed., pp. 177. New York: Praeger.

Howard, Michael. 1982. The Forgotten Dimension of Strategy. In *The Defense Policies of Nations,* D. J. Murray and P. R. Violti, eds. Baltimore: Johns Hopkins University Press.

Inbar, Efraim. 1982a. The American Arms Transfer to Israel. *Middle East Review* 15:45-48.

_____. 1982b. The Israeli Basement: With Bombs or Without? *Crossroads* 8:81-106.

_____. 1983. Israeli Strategic Thinking After 1973. *Journal of Strategic Studies* 6:32-49.

_____. 1984. Sources of Conflict Between Israel and the United States. *Conflict Quarterly* 4:56-65.

_____. 1985. Israel and Nuclear Weapons in the Post-1973 Period. In *Security or Armageddon: Israel's Nuclear Strategy,* Louis Rene Beres, ed. Lexington: Lexington Books.

Jordan, Robert S. 1976. United Nations General Assembly Resolutions as Expressions of Human Values. *International Studies Quarterly* 20:647-54.

Kang, Hoon. 1977. United States-South Korean Security Relations: A Korean Perspective. In *The Future of the Korean Peninsula,* Young C. Kim and Abraham M. Halpern, eds. pp. 167-81. New York: Praeger.

Kaplan, Morton A. 1957. *System and Process in International Politics.* New York: Wiley.

_____. 1970. *Great Issues of International Politics.* Chicago: Aldine.

Karsten, Peter. 1976. Response to Threat Perception: Accommodation as a Special Case. In *Historical Dimensions of National Security Problems,* E. Knorr, ed., pp. 158-59. Lawrence: University Press of Kansas.

Katz, Daniel. 1965. Nationalism and Strategies of International Conflict Resolution. In *International Behaviour,* H. C. Kelman, ed. pp. 354-90. New York: Holt, Rinehart & Winston.

Kedourie, Elie. 1980. A New International Disorder. *Commentary* 65:50-54.

Keohane, Robert O. 1969. Lilliputians' Dilemma: Small States in International Politics. *International Organization* 23:291-310.

_____. 1971. The Big Influence of Small Allies. *Foreign Policy* 1:16-82.

Kimche, David. 1973. *The Afro Asian Movement. Ideology and Foreign Policy of the Third World.* Jerusalem: Israel University Press.

Kissinger, Henry. 1965. *A Troubled Partnership.* New York: McGraw-Hill.

Klieman, Aaron S. 1970. Soviet Russia and the Middle East. *Studies in International Affairs* 4. Baltimore: Johns Hopkins University Press.

Knorr, Klaus E. 1956. *The War Potential of Nations. Princeton: Princeton* University Press.

_____. 1966. *On the Uses of Military Powers in the Nuclear Age.* Princeton: Princeton University Press.

_____. 1975. *The Power of Nations.* New York: Basic Books.

_____, ed. 1976. *Historical Dimensions of National Security Problems.* Lawrence: University of Kansas Press.

_____. 1977. On the International Uses of Military Force in the Contemporary World. *Orbis* 21:5-27.

Knorr, Klaus E. and Sidney Verba. 1961. *The International System.* Princeton: Princeton University Press.

Kochan, Ran, Susan A. Gitelson and Efraim Dubek. 1976. Black African Voting Behavior in the UN on the Middle East Conflict: 1967-72. In *Israel and the Third World,* M. Curtis and S. Gitelson, eds., pp. 289-317. New Brunswick: Transaction Books.

Korany, Bahgat. 1976. *Social Change, Charisma and International Behaviour: Toward a Theory of Foreign Policy-making in the Third World.* Geneva: A. W. Sijthoff-Leiden.

Laqueur, Walter, 1975. The West in Retreat. *Commentary* 60:44-52.

_____. 1980. Euro-Neutralism. *Commentary* 65:21-27.

LeoGrande, William M. 1980. Evolution of the Nonaligned Movement. *Problems of Communism* 29:33-52.

Levtzion, Nehemia. 1979. International Islamic Solidarity and Its Limitations. *Jerusalem Papers on Peace Problems* 29.

Lewis, Barnard. 1976. *The Return of Islam.* Commentary 61:33-49.

Li, Victor H. and John W. Lewis. 1977. Resolving the China Dilemma: Advancing Normalization, Preserving Security. *International Security* 2:11-24.

Liska, George. 1957. *International Equilibrium.* Cambridge: Harvard University Press.

Mannoni, Otare D. 1964. *Prospero and Caliban. The Psychology of Colonization. New York: Praeger.*

Maoz, Moshe. 1976. *The Image of the Jew in Official Arab Literature and Communications Media.* Jerusalem: Shazar Library.

Marcy, G. 1963. How Far Can Foreign Trade and Customs Agreements Confer Upon Small Nations the Advantages of Large Nations? In *Economic Consequences of the Size of Nations,* E.A.G. Robinson, ed., pp. 265-81. London: Macmillan.

Mates, Leo. 1972. *Nonalignment Politics and Current Policy.* Belgrade: Institute of International Politics and Economics.

Maynes, Charles W. 1983. Helping Japan on Defense. *New York Times,* April 20:27.

McBeath, Gerald. 1977. Taiwan in 1976: Chiang in the Saddle. *Asian Survey* 17:18-26.

McLane, Charles. 1973. Korea in Russia's East Asian Policy. In *Major Powers and Korea.* Young C. Kim, ed. Silver Spring: Research Institute on Korean Affairs.

Meddy-Weitzman, Bruce, 1981. *Arab Politics and the Islamabad Conference, January 1980.* Tel Aviv: Shiloach Institute.

Medzini, Meron. 1976. Asian Voting Patterns on the Middle East at the UN General Assembly. In *Israel and the Third World,* M. Curtis and S. Gitelson, eds. pp. 318-24. New Brunswick: Transaction Books.

Miller, John D. B. 1966. *The Politics of the Third World.* Oxford: Oxford University Press.

Modelski, George. 1961. Agraria and Industria. Two Models of the International System. In *The International System,* K. E. Knorr and S. Verba, eds., p. 122. Princeton: Princeton University Press.

Morgenthau, Hans. 1960. *The Purpose of American Politics.* New York: A. A. Knopf.

Moynihan, Daniel P. 1975. The United States in Opposition. *Commentary* 59:31-44.

——————. 1977. The Politics of Human Rights. *Commentary* 64:21.

——————. 1978. *A Dangerous Place.* Boston: Little, Brown.

——————. 1979. Further Thoughts on Words and Foreign Policy. *Atlantic Community,* Fall: 1-10.

Neustadt, Richard E. 1970. *Alliance Politics.* New York: Columbia University Press.

Nye, Joseph S. 1973. Regional Organizations and Peace. In *International Politics,* R. J. Art and R. Jervis, eds., pp. 130-58. Boston: Little, Brown.

Nyerrere, Julius K. 1977. America and South Africa. *Foreign Affairs* 55:671-84.

Oren, Nissan. 1980. The Fate of the Small in a World Concerted and in a World Divided. *Jerusalem Journal of International Relations* 5, 1:111-19.

Palestinian National Covenant. 1974. In *Palestinians and Israel,* Yehoshafat Harkabi, ed. Jerusalem: Keter.

Palmerston. 1954. In *The Struggle for Mastery in Europe, 1848-1918,* A.J.P. Taylor, ed. p. 147. Oxford: Clarendon Press.

Park, Robert E. 1928. Migration and the Marginal Man. *American Journal of Sociology* 33:881-93.

Peterson, M. J. 1982. Political Use of Recognition: The Influence of the International System. *World Politics* 34:324-52.

Plaut, Steven. 1980. Czechoslovakia 1938-Israel 1980. *Commentary* 70:23-27.

Podhoretz, Norman. 1976. The Abandonment of Israel? *Commentary* 61:23-31.

Porter, Gareth. 1979. Time to Talk with North Korea. *Foreign Policy* 34:52-73.

Quandt, William B. 1977. *A Decade of Decisions.* Berkeley: University of California Press.

Rabin, Itzhak. 1979. *The Rabin Memoirs.* Tel Aviv: Maariv Book Guild.

Reischauer, Edwin O. 1974. The Korean Connection. *The New York Times Magazine,* September 22: 15, 60, 63-64, 66, 68-69.

Rivlin, Benjamin. 1979. Middle East Issues at the Havana Nonalignment Summit. *Middle East Review* 12:40-44.

Rivlin, Benjamin and Jacques Fomerand. 1976. Changing Third World Perspectives and Policies Toward Israel. In *Israel and the Third World,* M. Curtis and S. Gitelson, eds. pp. 325-60. New Brunswick: Transaction Books.

Roberts, Adam. 1975. Do Economic Boycotts Ever Work? *New Society,* September 11:577-79.

Robinson, E. A. G., ed. 1963. *Economic Consequences of the Size of Nations.* London: Macmillan.

Roger, Robert F. 1975. Korea: Old Equation, New Factors. *Orbis* 19:116-17.

Rom, M. P. Yoseph. 1979. The Vietnamization of Israel. *Maariv,* September 10:9.

Rosenau, James N. 1971. Race in International Politics: A Dialogue in Five Parts. In *The Scientific Study of Foreign Policy,* J. Rosenau, ed., pp. 339-400. New York: Free Press.

Rothstein, Robert L. 1968. *Alliances and Small Powers.* New York: Columbia University Press.

Rubin, Barry. 1977. *International News and the American Media.* Washington Papers, Vol. 5, No. 49. Beverly Hills: Sage.

Rudolph, Lloyd I. and Susan Hoeber Rudolph. 1975. The Coordination of Complexity in South Asia—Summary Report. *Commission on the Organization of the Government Conduct of Foreign Policy,* Appendix V, 7:18. Washington, D.C.:U.S. Government Printing Office.

Safran, Nadav. 1978. *Israel, The Embattled Ally.* Cambridge: Harvard University Press.

Scheff, Thomas J. 1966. *Being Mentally Ill.* Chicago: Aldine.

Schelling, Thomas C. 1970. *Strategy of Conflict.* Cambridge: Harvard University Press.

Schurman, Franz. 1977. The Crisis Before Us. *The New York Times Book Review,* July 17:22.

Selya, Roger M. 1975. Trading Under Duress: The Case of Taiwan. *Asian Profile* 3:441-46.

Serfaty, Simon. 1981. The United States and Europe. *The Washington Quarterly* 4:70-86.

Shamir, Moshe. 1979. Cambodia—Now? *Maariv,* October 22:9.

Shapira, Yoram D. 1976. External and Internal Influences in Latin-American Israeli Relations. In *Israel and the Third World,* M. Curtis and S. Gitelson, eds., pp. 147-81. New Brunswick: Transaction Books.

Sheehan, Edward R. F. 1976. Step by Step in the Middle East. *Foreign Policy* 22:3-70.

Segev, Shmuel. 1984. Camp David Process is Dead. *Maariv,* January 27.

Shimoni, Yaakov. 1981. Israel and Europe. *The Jerusalem Quarterly* 19:92-107.

Shimoni, Yaakov and Evyatar Levine, eds. 1974. *Political Dictionary of the Middle East in the 20th Century.* New York: Quadrangle.

Shinn, Rinn-sup. 1973. Foreign and Reunification Policies. *Problems of Communism* 22:55-71.

Shurke, Astri. 1973. Gratuity or Tyranny: The Korean Alliance. *World Politics* 25:508-32.

Sicherman, Harvey. 1980a. The United States and Israel: A Strategic Divide? *Orbis* 24:381-94.

_____. 1980b. Western Europe and the Arab-Israeli Conflict. *Orbis* 24:845-57.

Simon, Herbert. 1957. *Models of Man.* New York: Wiley.

Singer, J. David and Melvin Small. 1966. The Composition and Status Ordering of the International System: 1815-1940. *World Politics* 18:236-82.

Slonim, Shlomo. 1974. United States-Israel Relations, 1967-73, A Study in the Convergence and Divergence of Interests. *Jerusalem Papers on Peace Problems,* No. 8. Jerusalem: Leonard Davis Institute for International Relations.

Speier, Hans. 1952. The Social Types of War. In *Social Order and the Risks of War,* H. Speier, ed. New York: George W. Stewart.

Steinberg, Bluma. 1977. Superpower Conceptions of Peace in the Middle East. *The Jerusalem Journal of International Relations* 2:70-82.

Taylor, A. J. P. 1954. *The Struggle for Mastery in Europe, 1848-1918.* Oxford: Clarendon Press.

Touval, Saadia. 1972. *The Boundary Politics of Independent Africa.* Cambridge: Harvard University Press.

Trice, Robert H. 1977a. Domestic Interest Groups and the Arab-Israeli Conflict. In *Ethnicity and United States Foreign Policy,* Abdul Aziz Said, ed., pp. 117-38. New York: Praeger.

_____. 1977b. Congress and the Arab-Israeli Conflict: Support for Israel in the United States Senate, 1970-73. *Political Science Quarterly* 92-443-63.

Triffin, R. 1963. The Size of the Nation and Its Vulnerability to Economic Nationalism. In *Economic Consequences of the Size of Nations,* E. A. G. Robinson, ed., pp. 248-65. London: Macmillan.

Truman, David B. 1951. *The Governmental Process: Political Interests and Public Opinion.* New York: A.A. Knopf.

Tucker, Robert W. 1972. *A New Isolationism: Threat or Promise?* New York: Universe Books.

_____. 1975. Egalitarianism and International Politics. *Commentary* 60:9-40.

Vital, David. 1967. *The Inequality of States.* Oxford: Clarendon Press.

_____. 1971. The Analysis of Small Power Politics. In *Small States in International Relations.* A. Schou and A. Brundtland, eds. pp. 15-28. Cambridge: Harvard University Press.

Wallace, Michael D. 1973. *War and Rank Among Nations.* Lexington: D. C. Heath.

Waltz, Kenneth N. 1967. International Structure, National Force and the Balance of World Power. *Journal of International Affairs* 21, 2:215-31.

Wildavsky, Aaron. 1977. What's In It For Us? America's National Interest in Israel. *Middle East Review* 10:5-13.

Willets, Peter. 1978. *The Nonaligned Movement.* London: Francis Pinter.

Wohlstetter, Albert. 1968. Illusions of Distance. *Foreign Affairs* 46:242-55.

Wolfers, Arnold. 1963. *Discord and Collaboration.* Baltimore: Johns Hopkins University Press.

Wood, Margaret M. 1963. *Paths of Loneliness.* New York: Columbia University Press.

Worsely, Peter. 1967. *The Third World.* London: Weidenfeld.

Wright, Quincy. 1964. *A Study of War,* abridged ed. Chicago: University of Chicago Press.

Zumwalt, Elmo R., Jr. 1980. Gorshkow and His Navy. *Orbis* 24:419-510.

# INTERNATIONAL STUDIES NOTES
## of the International Studies Association

*— a forum for conflicting views —*

INTERNATIONAL STUDIES NOTES is published to provide a challenging *multidisciplinary* forum for exchange of research, curricular and program reports on international affairs. It is designed to serve teachers, scholars, practitioners, and others concerned with the international arena.

*Recent and future topics include:* terror; science, technology and development; classroom simulations; human rights; local-global links; gaps between policymakers and academics; contradictory approaches to international affairs; summaries/comments on professional meetings.

Recent contributors have included Norman D. Palmer, David P. Forsythe, James N. Roseneau, Robert C. North, and Rose Hayden.

— RECOMMEND A SUBSCRIPTION TO YOUR LIBRARIAN —

INTERNATIONAL STUDIES NOTES of the International Studies Association is published quarterly by the University of Nebraska-Lincoln and the University of Wyoming and is edited by Joan Wadlow and Leslie Duly.

*Subscription Rates:* One year $20.00; two years $36.00.

Send subscriptions to: Leslie Duly, 1223 Oldfather Hall, University of Nebraska-Lincoln, Lincoln, Nebraska 68588.

# THE FLETCHER FORUM

## putting the pieces in place

Published in January and May each year, *The Fletcher Forum*
features articles on diplomacy, international law, politics
and economics, as well as shorter commentaries and book reviews.

☐ $9 One year — two issues
  (Foreign subscription) $13

☐ $17 Two years — four issues
  (Foreign subscription $24)

☐ $24 Three years — six issues
  (Foreign subscription $36)

☐ $15 Institutions — one year
  (Foreign institutions $20)

Send your payment to:  The Fletcher School of Law
                and Diplomacy
              Tufts University
              Medford, Massachusetts 02155

# Conflict

## All Warfare Short of War
### Edited by George K. Tanham

This quarterly journal focuses on conflicts short of formal war, including guerrilla warfare, insurgency, revolution, and terrorism. Articles also cover non-physical conflicts, such as those of an economic, social, political, and psychological nature. Issues will attempt to address some of the less visible and less publicized conflicts occurring in the world today.

*Selected Articles from the Fourth Volume of CONFLICT:*

Shattering the Vietnam Syndrome: A Scenario for Success in El Salvador

Liberation Theology in Latin America: Its Challenge to the United States

Unconventional Warfare: A Legitimate Tool of Foreign Policy

The Ethnic Factor in the Soviet Armed Forces

Soviet Nationalities in German Wartime Strategy 1941–1945

Managing the Ethnic Factor in the Russian and Soviet Armed Forces: An Historical Overview

The Soviet Union and Muslim Guerrilla Wars, 1920–1981: Lessons for Afghanistan

Soviet Central Asian Soldiers in Afghanistan

Tribal Marxism: The Soviet Encounter with Afghanistan

*Issued Quarterly Volume 5 $60.00*

## Crane, Russak & Company, Inc.
3 East 44th Street, New York, N.Y. 10017, (212) 867-1490

# CAIRO PAPERS IN SOCIAL SCIENCE
## بحوث القاهرة فى العلوم الاجتماعية

The CAIRO PAPERS IN SOCIAL SCIENCE provides a medium for the dissemination of research in social, economic and political development conducted by visiting and local scholars working in Egypt and the Middle East. Produced at the American University in Cairo since 1977, CAIRO PAPERS has published more than 20 issues of collected articles and monographs on a variety of topics. Beginning January 1983, issues will appear on a quarterly basis. Future topics include

     THE POLITICAL ECONOMY OF REVOLUTIONARY IRAN
     URBAN RESEARCH STRATEGIES FOR EGYPT
     THE HISTORY AND ROLE OF THE EGYPTIAN PRESS
     SOCIAL SECURITY AND THE FAMILY IN EGYPT
     THE NATIONALIZATION OF ARABIC AND ISLAMIC
         EDUCATION IN EGYPT: DAR AL-ULUM AND AL-AZHAR
     NON-ALIGNMENT IN A CHANGING WORLD

In addition, we plan to publish a special index of survey research conducted by Egyptian research centers and agencies which will be offered at a discount rate to our subscribers.

**************************************************************************
NAME:                           INSTITUTION:

ADDRESS:

CITY:                           STATE OR COUNTRY:


VOLUME SIX ORDERS
    INDIVIDUAL (US $15 or L.E.8)            INSTITUTIONAL (US $25 or L.E.10)
                                   Please indicate if standing order:
BACK ORDERS
    SINGLE ISSUES (US $4 or L.E.3)      _____VOLUME 4 (US $15 or L.E.8)
Please indicate title and author:



Enclosed is a check or money order for_____payable to THE AMERICAN UNIVERSITY IN CAIRO (CAIRO PAPERS).

Signature or authorization:

**************************************************************************
Inquiries or orders originating in the      Those originating elsewhere should
USA should be sent to:                       be sent to:

    CAIRO PAPERS IN SOCIAL SCIENCE          CAIRO PAPERS IN SOCIAL SCIENCE
    American University in Cairo            American University in Cairo
    866 U.N. Plaza                          P.O. Box 2511
    New York, N.Y. 10017                    Cairo, Egypt

Book format and printing
by
DEPARTMENT OF GRAPHICS
University of Denver